"The events of 2020 are revealing how each of us makes sense of important things like science, justice, uncertainty, authority, and Ultimate Reality. With his new book, Tim Elmore shows us his cards: wisdom and compassion for the next generation must take center stage. In The Pandemic Population, Tim tackles key moves caring adults can make—and helpful mindsets they can embrace—with and for children in turbulent times. It could be argued that The Pandemic Population is founded upon a belief in the phenomenal potential and promise of young people. Throughout this must read, Tim constantly inspires us to pay attention to the plans, feelings, and thoughts of young people, and he helpfully instructs us how to shepherd children wisely and kindly for such a time as this."

Tyler S. Thigpen Ph.D., Co-founder and head of The Forest School (www.theforest.school) and Institute for Self Directed Learning (www.sefldirect.school), and Faculty Chair at the University of Pennsylvania Graduate School of Education

"Understanding the impact of this pandemic on Generation Z is key to building them into vibrant leaders. This book will convince you our future can be bright!"

Sharlee Lyons, Director of The Larsen Leaders Academy at Purdue University; Principal The People Business

THE PANDEMIC
POPULATION

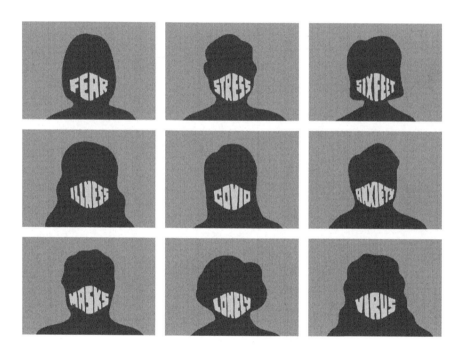

*Eight Strategies to Help Generation Z
Rediscover Hope After Coronavirus*

TIM ELMORE

Poet Gardener
PUBLISHING

Published in Atlanta, Georgia, by Poet Gardener Publishing in association with Growing Leaders, Inc.
www.GrowingLeaders.com

ISBN: 978-1-7320703-8-7
Printed in the United States of America

Library of Congress Cataloguing-in-Publication Data

Contents

This book is dedicated to all the people who haven't given up on kids.

ONE

Pandemics, Protests, and Panic Attacks: A History Defined by Tragedy

There is an age-old story that illustrates the state of millions of American teens today. It's the tale of a man who sat in a local diner waiting for his lunch. His countenance was down, he was feeling discouraged, and his tone was melancholy. When his waitress saw he was feeling low, she immediately suggested he go see Grimaldi. The circus was in town, and Grimaldi was a clown who made everyone laugh. The waitress was certain Grimaldi could cheer up her sad customer. Little did she know with whom she was speaking.

The man looked up at her and replied, "But, ma'am. I am Grimaldi."

In many ways, this is a picture of the Pandemic Population. On the outside, they're clowning around on Snapchat and TikTok, laughing at memes and making others laugh at filtered photos on social media. Inside, however, their mental health has gone south. It appears their life is a comedy, but in reality, it feels like a tragedy. They are mourning just how overwhelmed they feel—how behind they assume they are and how much they'll have to make up in order to catch up.

COMPLICATED AND COMPLEX

While our world has endured difficult eras in the past, including pandemics, world wars, famine and the like, the times in which we live are both complex and complicated. My colleague Steve Moore recently illustrated the difference between the two:

"*Complicated*" means a difficult situation stares you in the face. A student looking at a chalk board, trying to solve a math problem in class may find it complicated. Imagine, however, that student dozes off and naps for thirty minutes. When the student wakes up, the problem will still be there, but it will be unchanged. It is the same problem a half hour later. It's not harder or easier to solve.

"*Complex*" means a difficult situation that is constantly evolving stares you in the face. An air traffic controller at a commercial airport, who's helping planes take off and land, faces a tough challenge that doesn't stay the same. If she wakes up after a thirty-minute nap in the air tower, problems have gotten worse. What may have been complicated a half hour ago has now also become complex. It's a much tougher situation to solve.

The world that today's young people grow up in is both complex and complicated. It's a moving target, begging them to become both *resilient* and *resourceful*. And these two terms describe the meta-competencies they will need to thrive in the future. More on that later.

Our culture is anxious and the social world is marked by

- a rapid rate of change, often times fundamental change,
- complicated circumstances with multiple stakeholders,
- an ever-critical public eye that spots and posts every flaw,
- a virus that became a pandemic and shut everything down,
- a more educated populace who feels empowered by data,
- convoluted and nuanced interactions that are scrutinized constantly, and
- a fear of failing and an anxiety about the judgments of others around us.

Generation Z represents the population of young people who have no memories of the twentieth century, which millennials do have. Generation Z grew up in the twenty-first century when the world is different. While millennials grew up with cell phones, Generation Z grew up with smart phones. While millennials grew up with on-demand music on an iPod, Generation Z grew up with on-demand everything—almost every song, video, TV program, and movie is now "on demand." And while millennials are marked by September 11, 2001 as a tragic "rite of passage," Generation has endured daily, ongoing tragedies (i.e. mass shootings) capped off by the COVID-19 pandemic. The 9/11 tragedy was horrific, but it took place in specific locations (New York City or Washington DC), on a particular day that we could visit and grieve. (In fact, there is now a memorial at Ground Zero in Manhattan.) The coronavirus, on the other hand, has been a slow, sinister infection that has migrated around the world to multiple locations, stealing jobs and lives along the way. As the pandemic has taken its toll, one of the unexpected consequences was the cost to mental health. The effects of these difficult realities on Generation Z, which I am about to go over in detail, have been particularly impactful on a subset of this generation. These are the kids, young adults caught in a time of transition, who I now call the "Pandemic Population."

LIFE SINCE THE PANDEMIC POPULATION WAS BORN

Reflect with me on the first two decades of the twenty-first century. History pivoted as our world moved into a new millennium. Our world had already become complicated, and now it was becoming more complex as the final chapter of the 1990s concluded and we entered the year 2000. Walk with me down memory lane.

We began with the Y2K bug. This was a computer flaw many predicted would cause problems for hundreds of millions of people when dealing with dates beyond December 31, 1999. This Millennium bug led to a widespread scare, causing folks to buy food and water to stash away. When complex computer programs were first written in the 1960s, engineers used a two-digit code for the year, leaving out "19." As the year 2,000 approached, many felt systems would not interpret "00" correctly, causing a glitch in communication. While the solution was a simple fix to a four-digit number, Y2K revealed just how vulnerable people are to apocalyptic fears.

Next, there was the dot-com era bubble burst. By the end of the 1990s, many start-ups were launched by e-commerce entrepreneurs: their company was a store on a website, and their customers shopped online. During the dot-com bubble, the value of equity markets grew exponentially, with the technology-dominated Nasdaq index rising from under 1,000 to more than 5,000 between the years 1995 and 2000. In 2001 and 2002, the bubble burst, with equities entering a bear market. In the financial downturn, thousands lost jobs, money, and market share as companies went belly-up.

Next, we experienced a terrorist attack on September 11, 2001 that hit closer to home than any intrusion we'd ever experienced. Nineteen foreign terrorists hijacked jets over domestic soil and killed 2,974 people in New York, Washington DC, and Pennsylvania. It was the deadliest attack in our history. But it was only the beginning. After 9/11, our world experienced over 110,041 terrorist attacks between 2001 and 2017.[1] In the last decade, terrorists killed an average of 21,000 people worldwide each year,[2] creating a fearful culture for people in general and particularly for parents. The events of 9/11 sent us into an economic spiral, with both companies and nonprofit organizations going out of business.

Then, we witnessed a swelling number of scandals among large corporations, like Enron, Tyco, and WorldCom—companies millions had grown to trust and do business with. Each of these corporations had core values hanging on their walls that included "integrity" and "trust," but failed to practice them. We discovered that what's hanging on the wall is not nearly as important as what's happening down the hall, as my friend Andy Stanley likes to say.[3] Greed coerced leaders to hide poor decisions and bad transactions. Wall Street was perceived as corrupt, and this led to tighter legislation for businesses.

Next, we experienced the introduction of the smart phone, with iPhones and androids. At first these portable devices were marvels of entertainment and productivity, but over time, we began to experience both the addictive nature of these devices and the anxiety they foster: fear of missing out (FOMO), fear of being offline (FOBO) and fear of messing up (FOMU). Phones became essential yet they brought mental health consequences. A friend of mine once pointed out in conversation, when our phones had leashes, we were free. Now our phones are free, and we have leashes.[4]

Because most of us owned a smart phone, we next experienced the ubiquitous presence of social media. First, we added MySpace, then Facebook, Twitter, Instagram, WhatsApp and countless others. Over the last several years, more of them use images that disappear quickly, such as Snapchat and TikTok. Once again, the negative nature of social media surfaced when stories emerged about stalkers communicating with children and companies tracking our activity. More of us, even kids, have begun to prefer privacy and exclusivity with our posts. A typical teen has an Instagram account, but several "finsta" accounts (fake Instagram personas).

We also experienced the Great Recession of 2008 to 2009, which we were unprepared for. This financial downturn spawned the worst economy since the Great Depression of the 1930s, and it was the second downturn of the decade. The result? It devastated world financial markets as well as the banking and real-estate industries. The crisis led to increases in home-mortgage foreclosures worldwide and caused millions of people to lose their life savings, jobs, and homes. For many, it took years to recover, and some still have not.

Then, there were disputes against social injustice in the United States. Over the last decade, people have protested racial inequities, as people took sides on police brutality issues (#blacklivesmatter), gay and lesbian marriage rights (#lgbtrights), gun control issues (#marchforourlives), women's rights and sexual assault (#metoo)—all of which became movements in addition to topics for social media. Teenager Greta Thunberg became a spokesperson for global warming (#climatechange) as millions from Generation Z expressed confusion over why older adults failed to see the urgent problem. Regardless of where people stand on these issues, the interconnectedness of our world and the all-pervasiveness of social media makes these topics impossible to ignore.

The normalization of student loans became headline news as college tuition debt grew larger than credit card debt in the United States.[5] Millions of millennials still carry thousands of dollars of debt as they proceed through their careers, causing them to choose jobs merely because of the paycheck and not because of their giftedness or calling. As of 2019, college-tuition debt in America stood at $1.5 trillion and 42 million Americans carry part of that load, about one person in six.[6]

Next, we saw an increase in mass shootings in America. A mass shooting is defined as a shooting where four or more people are injured or killed.[7] In 2019, there were more mass shootings in the United States (417) than we had days in the year,[8] sparking a new debate on gun control and mental health. In a 2020 focus group I hosted, students in Atlanta acknowledged that whenever they hear a loud noise (like a pop) on campus, they duck. They're worried it's a gun going off. It has become normalized in the minds of teens today. And it has become another source of anxiety and panic attacks in America's youth.

In time, we witnessed the normalization of addictions in American life. From vaping to video games, pornography, social media, opioids, and other prescription drugs, many Americans found such coping mechanisms enabled them to endure their pain and anxiety. In fact, the twenty-first century became the period when legal addictions overtook illegal addictions[9] and addictive behavior became a growing topic among behavioral scientists. Most stunning of all, those struggling with addictions are often highly intelligent and educated professionals, meaning it isn't an intellectual issue but is likely an emotional one.

Along with these came political polarization. After having our first minority president, Barack Obama, we got the first complete outsider president—Donald Trump. These two men have very different approaches to leadership and politics. It was as though the political pendulum swung from one ideology to the other, where incredible gains were made for progressives first, followed by an equally incredible reaction from conservatives. As a kid, I remember Republicans and Democrats finding a way to work together in the 1970s. Today that seems unimaginable.

Mental health issues have reached epic proportions among Americans, especially young people. Once again, it is the normalization of anxiety, depression, and panic attacks. Anxiety is the most common mental-health disorder in the United States, affecting nearly one-third of both adolescents and adults, according to the National Institute of Mental Health.[10] "In its annual survey of students, the American College Health Association found a significant increase—to 62 percent in 2016 from 50 percent in 2011—of undergraduates reporting 'overwhelming anxiety' in the previous year."[11] Simultaneously, suicide attempts and completions also skyrocketed, causing US life expectancy to drop for the first time in decades.

In Spring of 2020, there was the coronavirus which sent us all home from work and school for months. By July 1, 2020, more than 10.3 million were infected and over 163,000 died around the world.[12] A record 6.6 million Americans applied for unemployment in one week.[13] By March 2020, no one questioned whether we'd be talking about this pandemic for generations. The only debate is—what do we compare it to? The

2008 financial crisis? September 11, 2001? World War II? As millions of people applied for unemployment in one week, some economists predicted it would compare to the Great Depression when unemployment hit 25 percent in America. In April 2020, the US unemployment rate jumped to nearly 15 percent (up from only 3.5 percent four months earlier) as 20.5 million people abruptly lost their jobs, according to the Labor Dept. By May 2020, half of the US population was not working.[14] It was a time of deep loss and poverty as we fought to recover from the global outbreak.

Finally, another season of protests crept up on all of us. After three murder cases made national news—Ahmaud Arbery, Breonna Taylor, and George Floyd, all unarmed black Americans who were killed by law-enforcement (or former) officers—our nation hit the streets in protest in major cities all over the country. Millions of people, many from Generation Z, protested racial injustice and specifically police brutality. While some of the protests turned violent, the damage and looting was mostly conducted by the hands of agitators and not genuine protestors. The protests went on daily for weeks and often police officers took a knee with protestors, joining hands with them and amplifying the message. While the scope was reminiscent of the 1960s protests, the unity between people was different than anything I'd seen before. Generation Z witnessed or participated in this firsthand.

What other notable factors have contributed to today's culture?

How Each Generation Might Respond to Our Current Crisis

Clearly, no individual can speak for their entire generation. Each of us are unique and possesses our own narrative on what's happening. But generations are defined by shared experiences, shared music, shared heroes, shared television programs, shared tragedies, shared economies, and shared moments. With that in mind, allow me to suggest what each generation might say if they could speak as a single person in response to the 2020 pandemic.

Silent Generation: "We've been through tough times before."
(not rattled)

These are senior citizens, the Silent Generation, born between 1929 and 1945. They're made up of people who survived the Great Depression and World War II. They feel they've seen it all and are now in their twilight years. They are not deeply rattled by COVID-19, unless they've been infected. My dad is a great example. Since he had invested in his retirement and is "sheltering in place"—just like he was before the nationwide quarantine.

Baby Boomers: "My retirement is disappearing."
(rattled)

These are the retiring or recently retired generation, who are seasoned veterans and now worry more about how they'll live on what they have saved. Less than half have reported saving enough to maintain their standard of living.[15] They are rattled because of this suboptimal reality, as well as because they're more vulnerable to the coronavirus.

Generation X: "Life is hard; steady as she goes."
(rattled a bit more)

Generation X (or the baby busters) are the smaller generation following the baby boomers whose generation launched with the introduction of the birth-control pill. All their lives, they've lived in the shadow of the boomers who are entering retirement age at a rate of 10,000 per day. Now they are in management and less worried about losing a job than a young professional. They know life is tough but still might feel vulnerable.

Millennials: "What will this do to my dreams?"
(rattled even more)

These young professionals in their 20s and 30s were caught between two economic downturns, one decade apart: the Great Recession (2008–2009) and the COVID-19 recession we're now experiencing. Because they grew up at a time when parents prized and praised them with trophies and accolades, this is a challenging time. The launch of their career has been far more difficult than any video game they played as a kid.

Generation Z: "I feel postponed and penalized."
(rattled a lot)

The youngest generation was already fraught with mental health issues and now has one more reason to feel angst and worry about the world. They grew up feeling overwhelmed by the thousands of social media posts they consume each day and now feel uncertain about their future prospects for internships, jobs, financial independence, and home ownership. Oh and not to mention, their personal physical and emotional health.

It's difficult to imagine what it would feel like to be an adolescent today—a high school or college student who's coming of age at a time when even the adults are divided about how to handle the virus and when to return to work and are unable to make any predictions for their future. What I do believe, however, is that past generations who survived and even thrived after a global tragedy, be it a world war, a famine, or a pandemic, did so because they were guided well by their leaders and instilled with hope, belief, and grit.

This is our challenge today.

DID WE BUILD SNOWFLAKES OR SNOWMEN?

Some of my colleagues have concluded: *Well, the Coronavirus is bad, but we've been through bad experiences before. Tragedies strike in nearly every generation as they grow up.* While this is true, today is different because adults may not have done an adequate job of building grit and resilience in the emerging generation. Let's face it, most of us find it difficult to delay gratification, to work hard at something when we see no quick return, to receive hard feedback from others, or to bounce back when we've failed. Our world is "on demand" and "instant access," and has produced "Google reflexes," where Alexa or Siri immediately respond to our requests. As I meet over ten thousand parents at events each year, I wonder if we're part of our kids' problem.

For years, journalists, educators, and employers described Generation Z in America as a "snowflake generation." Why? Because so many of these kids have been raised in a delicate, soft environment protected from life's harsh realities and responsibilities. Some even wrote that we've coddled them, protecting them with bubble wrap."

The term *snowflake* has been used to refer to children raised by their parents in ways that give them an inflated sense of their own uniqueness. Initially, the term *snowflake generation* was mere slang, but was soon listed as one of *Collins Dictionary*'s 2016 words of the year. *Collins* defines the term as "the young adults of the 2010s, viewed as being less resilient and more prone to taking offence than previous generations".[16] Later the *Financial Times* included *snowflake* in their annual Year in a Word list, defining it as "a derogatory term for someone deemed too emotionally vulnerable to cope with views that challenge their own, particularly in universities and other forums once known for robust debate."[17]

How and Why Did These Snowflakes Appear?

Helicopter Parents

These are the parents we've read about since 2002, who hover over their children, ensuring they get all the benefits they deserve. More than thirty years ago, parenting styles began to shift. Moms and dads became preoccupied with the safety, status, and self-esteem of their kids. As this parenting population grew, culture began to reflect their sentiments: Baby on Board signs in the back of the minivan, thousands of new parenting and self-help books, and child-safety rules displayed in parks and daycare centers. In the name of "helping our kids," parents did their child's homework, hovered over them at soccer practice, and joined their graduate at his first job interview. I would say in some places, the "helicopter" has become an "apache helicopter."

Participation Ribbons and Trophies

Eventually, youth sports leagues felt it was important to celebrate participation more than wins. It was understandable. Most kids won't win a championship, and adults felt that should not prevent those average players from being rewarded in some way. A few years ago, I visited a friend's home and saw his child's room filled with trophies and ribbons his child had been given. He had never won any championships. Celebrating participation has fostered an expectation of rewards just for showing up. It did not prepare kids for the world that awaits them.

Grade Inflation

Student's grades have been on the rise for over forty years—not so much because they are smarter than children decades ago, but because grades have been inflated by schools. In the 1960s, the average grade given was a C. Why? Because C means average. Today, the average grade is an A. Many adults fear students cannot handle the harsh reality of a C. I spoke in one school district where faculty told me they were not allowed to use red ink when grading papers because it was too harsh. Some told me they were not permitted to use the word "no" because it was too negative.

Virtual Realities and Prescribed Activity

Instead of making teens work jobs, we got them involved with recitals, practices and games—all supervised and prescribed by adults of course. While piano, ballet, and sports can begin to cultivate personal discipline, these activities are still virtual realities, only a facsimile of the real world. The stakes aren't real. When a teen says they want to do something that actually matters, adults place them in a supervised program that emulates the real world. It's all controlled by adult leaders, which fosters dependency and reduces ownership. We conditioned them to need us, and now we laugh at them for bringing mom to the job interview.

Technology and the Media

As this generation grew up over the last twenty years, portable devices and social media took over. Kids today are exposed to thousands of images each day, often causing them to feel jealous over what friends are doing (having seen their Instagram posts) and believing everyone deserves the latest smart device, the latest Madewell jeans, the latest Xbox, the latest Nike shoes, and a subscription to Netflix. Entitlement and materialism usually walk hand in hand.

Safe Places in College

As students enter college, they begin to clamor for safe places, free from opposition or harsh feedback. This came to light in a confrontation between Yale University students and the faculty head of college, Nicholas Christakis. The confrontation arose after Christakis' wife, Erika, a university lecturer, suggested students should "relax a bit rather than labeling fancy dress Halloween costumes as culturally insensitive." This sparked a "screaming, almost hysterical mob of students."[18] Even if their views are right, the answer isn't always to remove opposition. It's to know how to handle it.

On top of all of this, today we live in the aftermath of the COVID-19 pandemic, which has swept the world off of its feet, just when these same young adults were coming of age. When teens look to their parents, teachers, coaches, or employers, they see an adult population uncertain about how to handle the situation because we've never faced it before either. We've often led with fearful paradigms and scarcity mindsets, which further deepens the angst of Generation Z. It's a perfect storm of external and internal forces that have put us all in a vulnerable mental state.

WHO'S TO BLAME?

In the end, far too often these "snowflakes" are products of our making. Not seeing what was happening soon enough, parents, teachers and other adults forgot that raising children is not just about *protecting* but is also about *preparing*. We wouldn't let them fail. We removed the consequences of poor decisions. We praised the wrong qualities in them. We risked too little, we rescued too quickly, and we raved too easily.[19] As they came of age and should have been ready to enter adulthood—more educated and with greater advantages than past generations—a mammoth percentage moved home after graduation. A 2010 study revealed that a full one-third of American males between the ages of twenty-two and thirty-four still lived at home with their parents.[20] While the challenge involves all genders, our males have been the greatest victims of this tragedy. They often remained boys when it was time to become men. For instance, while males and females both move home after college, the women often return home with a plan. The men usually return home with no plan at all. Their *Call of Duty* video game becomes a stand-in for real life success, and Mom is often far too willing to cook, clean, and cater to them.

In this unique period in history, we must develop grit and resilience in Generation Z and particularly this subset among this generation whom we call the Pandemic Population.

So, let's talk about how we get started.

Talk It Over

1. When you consider your students, what seems to be informing their narrative on life?

2. How has culture played a role in how they think? How about school or family?

3. In what ways have you aided in a wrong or unhealthy perspective in your children or students?

TWO

What We Can Learn About Generation Z from the Silent Generation

In a 1948 speech to the House of Commons, Winston Churchill—paraphrasing a quote from George Santayana—said, "Those who fail to learn from history are condemned to repeat it."[21]

So, let's learn from history.

About a century ago, the world faced one of our most devastating pandemics, lasting from 1918 to 1920. It was called the Spanish flu, or the influenza pandemic. It was said to have infected an estimated 500 million people—about a third of the global population—and claimed an estimated 20 to 50 million lives. This flu was first spotted in Europe and carried over the Atlantic Ocean to America when soldiers returned home after World War I. Many called it the Spanish flu because Spain was especially hit hard. It spread so rapidly that it ambushed most countries. At the time, there were no effective drugs or vaccines to treat that flu strain. Like today, "citizens were ordered to wear masks; schools, theaters and businesses were shuttered and bodies piled up in makeshift morgues before the virus ended its deadly global march."[22] In fact, during this pandemic, "the New York City health commissioner tried to slow the transmission of the flu by ordering businesses to open and close on staggered shifts to avoid overcrowding on the subways."[23]

The US census bureau has conducted a National Health Interview Survey (NHIS) annually for decades. When economist Craig Garthwaite studied the results, he compared the NHIS respondents' health conditions to the dates when their mothers were probably exposed to the flu. *The Atlantic* explains:

Children born during the pandemic grew into shorter, poorer, less educated adults with higher rates of physical disability than one would expect. Chances are that none of Garthwaite's flu babies ever knew about the shadow the pandemic cast over their lives. But they were living testaments to a brutal truth: Pandemics— even forgotten ones—have long-term, powerful aftereffects.[24]

So, while death is common from influenza, it's uncommon to see it in the volume our world endured a century ago. After the Spanish flu pandemic, the United States entered a recession between 1920 and 1921, then evolved into the "roaring 20s" with new fashions, new dances, and a touch of audacity. Little did they know, a crisis of a different sort was on the horizon.

THE SILENT GENERATION

One decade later, beginning in late 1929, a new population of kids began to be born, kids who would grow up learning life's hardest lessons earlier than most generations did because they would endure an economic depression—officially called the Great Depression—such as our nation has never seen since. It began with a stock market crash in November 1929, that led thousands of Americans to make a run on their bank to withdraw their cash. Because this was before any regulations existed on insurance, the banks were unready for such a withdraw. Many closed their doors. As the economy spiraled downward, hard times rose. Companies let employees go, and many went out of business. Folks learned to get by on less and share resources with one another. While the economic downturn hit hardest between 1929 and 1933, unemployment remained high for the entire decade.[25] Many historians and economists believe the Great Depression didn't officially end until we entered World War II in 1941.

My parents are part of this generation. My mother passed away fifteen years ago, far too early in my opinion. I still miss her to this day. My father continues on, turning 90 in 2020. He was born in 1930 so the first fifteen years of his life were marked by the Great Depression and World War II. He learned to be frugal and grateful. He carried a "waste not, want not" attitude into the twenty-first century. Some of the daily signals of this attitude for me as a child were the same that many with Great Depression parents will remember:

- "Turn the lights off when you leave the room. It'll save electricity."
- "Shut the door when you leave the house. We're not air-conditioning the neighborhood."
- "Keep that paper bag and rubber band. We may need it someday."
- "Why not just have leftovers tonight? There's no need to go out."
- "You can wear hand-me-downs one more year, can't you?"
- "Remember, enjoying a Coca-Cola is a special treat."
- "Save that wrapping paper (at Christmas), we can use it next year!"

These sentiments are a subtle aftereffect of growing up as a child during the Great Depression. When I speak to my dad about this period of his life, he confirms that those years were tough times financially. At the same time, however, he believes they were the best years of his life. Often he will tell stories of how everyone looked out for one another in his neighborhood, sharing milk and cheese and meat, and offering others job when they any to give.

In fact, I interviewed two dozen "Great Depression kids," all in their 80s and 90s to discover if there were commonalities in their earliest experiences. I wondered what pattern may have existed that informs how we lead kids today, during this deep economic downturn. My interviews included my in-laws, Jay (90) and Jackie (88) Hobson, and my dad, Skip Elmore (89). Here is what I found.

1. The majority of them were not aware they were living in the Great Depression.

Because there was no social media or 24-7 news cycle in the 1930s, most kids could tell life was tough, but did not feel as if they were victims of horrible times. They saw that mom and dad were struggling to provide food, clothes, and necessities, but that seemed normal, not unusual. When asked if they even knew about the "Great Depression" when they were kids many replied, "Oh, heavens no." By and large, adults helped their young retain an innocence in the midst of hardship. One suggested that enduring those tough times may have prepared Americans mentally for World War II.

2. Everyone felt they were all the same and were in this thing together.

There didn't seem to be a "comparison trap" among families in the 1930s like we have today. Today we might be very aware of the vacations others enjoy, the clothes they own, or the food they consume, thanks to posts on social media, but ninety years ago, that didn't happen. Not surprising, not knowing seemed to have helped them emotionally handle their lack. Think about it this way: if you were to grow up impoverished in a wealth city like Los Angeles, you'd be much more likely to feel like a victim, than if you had grown up with the same level of wealth in a state like Iowa or Ohio. Why? In Los Angeles, an income discrepancy is obvious, while in Iowa or Ohio, it would be harder to notice. So much of our feelings about our wealth is relative; our opinion of our own status is often determined by how we compare ourselves to others.

3. People maintained simplicity, gratitude, and contentment.

I was struck by how many Great Depression kids spoke of how little it took to make them happy. One recalled that Saturday night entertainment was walking through town after the stores closed to "window shop." No buying, just looking. That was a highlight from their weekend that they still remember to this day. Another noted that while more people lived in town, they retained their "farm habits," enabling them to grow gardens for food and trim their grocery bill. One mentioned that church members all grew vegetables, then brought what they grew to the church basement to share with one another. They all recalled saving everything, from rubber bands to plastic bags.

4. Adults raised kids collectively and worked to build morals and work ethic.

Yesteryear, an entire neighborhood of parents raised the kids. One child from the Great Depression recalled his mother marching him down to the store when he won a free candy bar in a contest, believing he may have stolen or gambled for it. Adults tended to back each other up in such times to ensure kids learned ethics. Several said they had moms that always saw the positive side of life—singing songs, reading books to neighbor kids, and rarely, if ever, complaining. It was common to borrow flour or butter from neighbors. They recalled adults talking on the porch over a glass of lemonade, discussing how to raise children who were humble but not hungry. Adults trained kids to be *self-sufficient* yet *interdependent, frugal* yet *charitable*—an interesting mix that seems to be missing today.

5. Good attitudes and virtues seemed to be paramount.

Every adult reinforced maintaining a positive attitude. There was a sense of *community responsibility*, and complainers were frowned upon. There was a collective sense that you should not feel entitled to special perks or embrace a victim mindset. Even though toilet paper was relatively new, no one hoarded it. They lived by the mindset "only take what you need." In fact, if you had extra, you gave it to someone who didn't have it. Children in a family often shared one bike. Selfishness was a no-no. Children were taught to think "long term." Planning, frugality, and conservatism were celebrated virtues. Saving more than spending; generosity not hoarding; humility not cockiness, service over selfishness. What's mine is yours.

As I reflect on how differently this generation handled their lack, it strikes me that these are the same life lessons we must pass on to Generation Z.

Have you noticed any other life lessons from members of the Silent Generation you know?

LESSONS LEARNED FROM THIS GENERATION

Since millions among the Silent Generation lived long lives and became good citizens decades later (my parents included), we can learn a lot from them about Generation Z, who is growing up in similar times. In fact, consider for a moment some similarities:

The Silent Generation (1929–1939)	Generation Z (2001–2020)
• Two economic slumps	• Three economic slumps
• Suicide rates increased	• Suicide rates increased
• Food became scarce for millions	• Meat became scarce for millions
• Unemployment rose to 25%	• Unemployment rose to nearly 15%

After listening to a focus group of elders (all over 80 years old) and interviewing senior citizens at Mount Miguel Covenant Village (a retirement center in San Diego), I noticed three negative and six positive outcomes from their recollection of the Great Depression. Let's look together at both the negative and the positive and see what there is to learn. The negative results were an increase in suicide rates, risk aversion, and lower expectations.[26]

First, of the six primary causes of death a hundred years ago, only suicides increased during the Great Depression. Suicide mortality peaked (along with unemployment) during the worst years of the recession: 1921, 1932, and 1938.[27] In other words, we learned that economic depression can and often does trigger emotional depression.

Second, risk aversion showed up in the daily habits of everyday Americans for years following the Great Depression. It took decades for people to regain consumer confidence, to plan without fear of another period of scarcity, and to take risks in their careers. Many retained the outlook "just be grateful you have a job." Children of the Great Depression were wary of the stock market for their entire lives.[28]

Third, it became natural for this generation who grew up with less material possessions and luxuries to enter adulthood with lower expectations. When people are formed by living simply, it's quite natural for them to be minimalists and have fewer demands even when times are economically better. Standards of living certainly went up for my parent's generation, but they tended to remain satisfied with a simple life. Although I grew up in an upper-middle class neighborhood, I recall my mother hanging paper towels on the clothesline for them to dry so we could use them again. We didn't expect to have fresh paper towels or new napkins for every meal.

While it may seem to you that the negative effects of the Great Depression might rest firmly in the past, as it turns out, there is evidence that these same realities are present today in Generation Z. Two generations almost a century apart show the same warning signs.

May I connect the dots for you?

Today, young people are dying from suicide at record rates. The suicide rate among people aged 10 to 24 increased 56 percent between 2007 and 2017, according to a new report by the Centers for Disease Control and Prevention.[29] While the majority of suicides during the Great Depression were adults, today it's the youngest population who lead the trend. The prevalence of social media today, combined with 24-7 real-time reporting of all the news occurring around the world, has meant that Generation Z is exposed to the world's challenges all too early. Kids can consume it as soon as they get a smart phone.

Risk aversion seems to mark young people as well. "They were impressionable kids during the crash of 2008, when many of their parents lost their jobs or their life savings or both," writes journalist Adam Piore.[30] They are not looking to take many risks. In fact, that's a growing trend among millennials and Generation Z. "In a 2019 survey of University of Georgia students, the career office found the most desirable trait in a future employer was the ability to offer secure employment."[31] Generation Z members are looking for security and certainty. Why? Because they haven't had much certainty in their lives up to this point.

Expectations have also shifted. While some among Generation Z still assume they will build an app and become a millionaire by the time they're thirty, millions more have lowered their expectations for their post-graduation life. The university student focus groups I've hosted reveal their newfound belief that life will be harder for them. Many expect that their job prospects will be fewer and more difficult to find after COVID-19, and that they may not own a home for decades, due to tuition debt. Students said things like "It's just sad what we're going through" and "I feel like my graduation is finally here and all my preparation means nothing. I have to start all over."

So, how do we reduce these negatives and ensure Generation Z changes their trajectory? To find the answer, I believe we must look to the positive characteristics of the Silent Generation.

Pursuing Positive Outcomes

Fortunately, there were a larger number of positive effects, even virtues, that continue to show up in our oldest population who were raised in the Great Depression. Whether the connection between these virtues and the times they were raised in is a causality or a correlation, I find it interesting how often these characteristics appear in our senior citizens. I believe we could and should target these same outcomes as we lead Generation Z.

Consider this fact: the Silent Generation was also given the title the "Builder Generation," primarily because they were in charge of reconstruction after the war. They learned to build something out of very little or nothing at all. As I interviewed members of the Builder Generation, I began to see predictable patterns. There are at least six beliefs I spotted in my case sample.

Beliefs of The Builder Generation

1. **Be humble.**
   One of the consistent virtues of these depression kids was humility. They realize they are but smaller pieces of a large puzzle; very little arrogance or cockiness remains in them.

2. **Be grateful.**
   They are appreciative of the people who played a part in their progress. They realize that while they worked hard, they did not achieve their goals alone.

3. **Be a good worker.**
   Work ethic is a staple for senior citizens. Even if they felt they weren't great models of an industrious spirit, they still knew it was the barometer for a quality employee.

4. **Be kind.**

They learned to look out for each other during the dark days of the Depression and World War II. They're marked by the acts of service between neighbors in their earliest memories.

5. **Be resilient.**

Enduring several society setbacks while they grew up, these Depression kids had to learn to bounce back after hardship. Grit and resilience were normal and expected.

6. **Be resourceful.**

Because most didn't enjoy lots of resources between 1929 and 1945, they had to learn to be resourceful. They made much out of little and discovered how to make life work on less.

In 2013, Ardyth Stull wrote a graduate dissertation called, "Stories of the Children of the Great Depression: What I Learned From My Parents." This thesis provides quantitative and qualitative research from interviews she did with Great Depression kids, offering what we can learn about the values adults embraced during the Great Depression that enabled them to provide for the physical and emotional needs of their families during economic hardship. She wrote,

> *I was surprised to discover the fond memories and good experiences that were shared, despite the fact that all the participants' families had endured hardships. The Great Depression was difficult, but not devastating for most of them. I asked if they realized they were living during the Great Depression when they were children. Several spoke at once and said they did not, stating that "everyone was the same. We didn't know any different."*[32]

One of the fascinating outcomes of poor economies is that they can cultivate both people who are risk-averse and those who are entrepreneurs. My dad was an entrepreneur, going into business for himself with his brother, Gene. They built a solid business in San Diego, assembling security cameras for stores and other outlets to prevent shoplifting and vandalism. They met a need and the business grew up the coast of California before they sold it and retired. Thanks to their resourcefulness and resilience, the Builder Generation spawned millions of entrepreneurs in the workforce.

What other qualities did this generation model for future generations?

WHY IS GENERATION Z NOT EXPERIENCING THESE SAME POSITIVE TRAITS TODAY?

Since we found common negatives traits between the Silent Generation and Generation Z, it would be natural to assume that we would also find similar positive traits. Sadly, that isn't the case.

In former generations who experienced hardships, young people emerged afterward with a growth narrative inside them. By this I mean that following the economic downturn, the world war, or the high death toll of a pandemic, the struggle seemed to have made them *better* not *bitter*. The story they told afterward was a positive one: We survived. We must be strong. The future is bright. They developed a "growth mindset" instead of a "fixed mindset" as Dr. Carol Dweck teaches. When we step back and view the pages of history, we recognize that more important than the tough times people endure is the narrative they form in their minds about those tough times.

So, what will Generation Z's narrative be?

While each individual is able to form his or her own personal narrative, a society tends to form a collective narrative that defines the times. Like a good movie, it becomes the soundtrack behind the scenes, and as with any soundtrack, it can be melancholy, adventurous, upbeat, or even downright depressing. Frequently, the authors of this soundtrack are the poets of our times—the musicians. They're the ones who put music and lyrics together, creating shared narratives that describe how we all feel at the time. For example, the rock and roll of the 1960s and 1970s adequately articulated the rebellious times in which they were written. They are the perfect soundtrack for the demonstrations, assassinations, and protests that marked the era. During the 80s and early 90s, musicians like Kurt Cobain of Nirvana and Marilyn Manson gave lyrics to the jaded and even cynical spirit of Generation X.

Today's Billboard Hot 100 songs reflect another turn toward sadness, negativity, and anxiety. These songs influence Generation Z, using minor keys and slower rhythms. It's quite fascinating and revealing. Just take a look at the narrative transformation of these popular songs from the last several years. I've chosen ones that illustrate the trend that's occurring across a broad scale:

2004 — "Let's Get It Started" by the Black Eyed Peas

This hit song has an upbeat tempo, the tone is confident, and the lyrics make you want to dance. In fact, the music video is several young men and woman dancing in the streets at night:

> *Burn it till it's burnt out,*
> *Turn it till it's turned out*
> *Act up from north, west, east and south*
> *Everybody, everybody, let's get into it, get stupid*
> *Get it started, get it started, get it started*
> *Let's get it started in here*[33]

2015 — "Stressed Out" by Twenty One Pilots

Just over a decade later, this Grammy—award winning song is musically upbeat, but the music video surrounds images of a young man riding a big wheel trike and returning to his childhood home. The lyrics center on wishing we could go back to simpler times:

> *I was told when I was older all my fears would shrink,*
> *But now I'm insecure and I care what people think.*
> *My name's Blurryface and I care what you think…*
> *Wish we could turn back time, to the good old days*
> *When our mamas sang us to sleep—but now we're stressed out.*[34]

2018 — "Sick Boy" by Chainsmokers

By this time, the acknowledgment of our mental health issues is blatant—no stigmas. The lyrics admit to narcissism and sickness and how we value our lives based on the responses we get on social media:

Don't believe the narcissism where everyone projects and expects
*   you to listen to 'em,*
Make no mistake I live in a prison that I made myself, it is my
*   religion.*
And they say that I am a sick boy,
Easy to say when you don't take the risk boy
Welcome to the narcissism where we're united under our
*   indifference.*
Feed yourself with my life's work,
How many likes is my life worth?[35]

2019 — "Pajamas" by Gnash

This song was released last year, a total and blatant admittance to the fact that our world has grown so mad and so sad. Perhaps the best response to our "bad world," Gnash determines, is to stay home in our pajamas. This was a prophetic utterance, one year before the COVID-19 pandemic:

Let's watch TV with the sound off, 'cause the news is always bad,
Let's be immature and ignorant, 'cause I don't feel like being sad.
I don't know what the point is, just know I've been disappointed
Each night and every moment—and I don't want to play no
*   more:*
Let's stay in our pajamas, let's not leave the house...[36]

2019 — "Bury a Friend" by Billie Eilish

Billie Eilish won five Grammys in 2020, including best album, best song, and best new artist. She is a Generation Z teen, whose songs about dark topics are extremely popular. When she released her award-winning album, "When We All Fall Asleep, Where Do We Go?" it was downloaded 194 million times in the first week. The song "Bury a Friend" offers listeners harsh, even suicidal lyrics:

Step on glass, staple your tongue.
Bury a friend, try to wake up.
Cannibal class, killing the son,
Bury a friend, I want to end me.[37]

Journalist and music critic, Monica Moser writes of Billie Eilish,

> *It's not even that she's writing about really dark and twisted*
> *things—she's allowing her young audience to go to this dark place*
> *with her and feel okay about being there....*
>
> *What if I was so immersed in her album when I was going*
> *through some of the hardest and most confusing things I've ever*
> *gone through in my formative years? I would not feel comforted,*
> *uplifted, or reached. I would feel pushed further and forcibly into*
> *my own darkness.*[38]

Can you hear the narrative soundtrack of Generation Z now?

What Are Today's Poets Telling Us?

I selected these songs not because they make my point but because they seem to depict the youth culture that I am already hearing in my conversations with Generation Z. It appears that the youth narrative is trending negative. Even still, I admit that these songs are an anecdotal sampling of the millions of new songs available to us today. To get the full picture, let's look at the numbers to see how today's "poets" have written songs that both reflect and direct the narrative of Generation Z.

Alberto Acerbi is an anthropologist who wrote a book in 2019 called *Cultural Evolution in the Digital Age*. In the book, Acerbi and his team examine the positive and negative emotions in song lyrics from 150,000 songs, including the Billboard Hot 100 chart, from 1965 to 2015. His discoveries were revealing:

- Song lyrics have become measurably more sad in the last fifty years.

- In 1965, about 450 negative-emotion words were used in popular music; in 2015, that number was above 700, a growth trend of more than a third.

- In 1965, over 1,750 positive-emotion words were used; by 2015, the positive words dropped to 1,150, again a decline of about a third.

- The effect can be seen even when we look at single words. The usage of the word love, for example, was cut in half over fifty years, going from about four hundred to two hundred instances. The word hate, on the contrary, which until the 1990s was not even mentioned in any top 100 songs, is now used somewhere between twenty and thirty times a year.[39]

Interestingly, the tone and tempo of songs has also shifted. Researchers in the UK analyzed 500,000 songs written between 1985 and 2015 and found a similar decrease in "happiness" and "brightness" subjects coupled with an increase in "sadness." When they analyzed the tone of the Billboard Hot 100 songs, they found that minor keys and tonalities (those perceived as gloomier) increased. The hit songs have also become slower in tempo.[40] There seems to be an association of today's listeners being more savvy and educated while also being more cynical and jaded. If ignorance is bliss—to be savvy must mean to be melancholy. Unfortunately, this is the narrative of today's typical teen, and it all started before the COVID-19 pandemic.

Have you witnessed your students drawing their perspectives from today's "poets"?

What's the Secret to Changing the Narrative?

As we've seen, although there are similarities in the hardships faced between the Silent Generation and Generation Z, there are remarkable differences in the outcomes. The deciding factor in this change, as we've seen, is the narrative with which each generation engaged the challenges they faced. When the Silent Generation faced hardship, they were encouraged to be resilient, resourceful, and respectful. When Generation Z faced similar hardships, they were encouraged to be savvy, cynical, and stoic. If we want to change the outcome, we've got to change how we lead Generation Z through the challenges they face.

Developmental psychologist Emmy Werner introduced research on children's resilience. Emmy herself was a child during World War II in Europe and survived horrible circumstances there. As an adult, Werner studied the letters, journal entries, and diaries of two hundred child eye-witnesses, then held in-depth interviews with adult survivors to learn about their experiences. In her book *Through the Eyes of Innocents*, she writes that many of the kids became adults who held "an extraordinary affirmation of life."[41]

There were four big takeaways Werner found that made the difference in these children.

1. Limited amount of exposure

The kids who were exposed to lots of calamity for many hours fared worse; the ones who had a limited amount early on, fared better. Today, too much media coverage can be harmful to kids. "A study of the Oklahoma City bombings found that middle school children who watched repeating loops of television coverage were more likely to have symptoms of PTSD seven weeks later (even though none of their families were harmed), compared to children who watched less television coverage."[42] I believe we must put boundaries on the amount of news "loops" our kids watch. The key? Watch thirty to sixty minutes of news updates and get on with your day.

2. Loving caregivers

Not surprisingly, a caring adult offering support was a game changer for how the kids turned out as adults. Anna Freud, Sigmund Freud's daughter, reported on children who survived the Nazi Blitz in England in a book she coauthored called *War and Children*. These kids had adults who led them intentionally, encouraged them, and offered emotional guidance. The good news is—the adult doesn't have to be a parent. A teacher, aunt, coach, sibling, neighbor, or counselor can provide the essential care kids need. The key is a trusted adult was present to offer guidance and support. Today, the same is true. We must offer clear guidance, emotional support, and encouragement.

3. Calm leadership

"When uncertainty or danger strikes, children are "wired" to look to their caregivers to interpret how safe they should feel. If their primary adult is calm, a child feels reassured. But if their adult is upset, the child feels unsafe, and their body and brain go into threat mode. When the threat system is on too long without relief, physical and mental health problems can result."[43] The key is for kids to have an adult who continues normal routines that provide security and order amidst what may feel like chaos. Playing games. Doing chores. Eating meals. Sleeping on schedule. Recent research finds that the presence of a calm adult can even reduce levels of cortisol, the stress hormone, in a child's body.[44] This means that you as their leader must practice self-care so you are ready to offer calm leadership in a time of uncertainty.

4. Higher calling

Finally, Werner's research shows that adult leaders who embrace faith in a "higher power" were able to guide kids into more resilient responses after a calamity. Many studies of resilience find that survivors who do well have strong philosophies or spiritual traditions. "Ann Masten, professor at the Institute for Child Development at the University of Minnesota, writes in her book, *Ordinary Magic: Resilience in Development*, that most faith traditions incorporate the ingredients for resilience." Further, "recent psychological work suggests that having a sense of purpose helps, too. When children are able to pitch in and contribute—in their families or their community—they develop mastery, they feel valued, and their confidence grows."[45]

My question is, Are you providing this kind of leadership to the Pandemic Population?

An Identity Forged in Hardship

While, today's tough times are not identical to the Great Depression, this cohort of young people are certainly stepping into a more uncertain world than most graduates have in the past several decades. For young people all over the world, hand sanitizer and masks have replaced caps and gowns, social distancing has replaced hangout time, and anxiety has replaced excitement about the future.

My friend Leah Farish says,

> *This age group will have experienced apartness from peers in a way that will set them apart from other age groups. This connected generation disconnected, at least regarding in-person interactions. And this may play a role in the story they tell themselves. In fact, it could be a legitimate excuse for them falling behind socially or emotionally as the enter adulthood. If…that's what they allow to shape their story.*

Leah reminds us,

> *Biographers note that long periods of isolation in childhood have contributed to the greatness of figures such as Teddy Roosevelt, John F. Kennedy, Helen Keller, Winston Churchill, Mikhail Baryshnikov, Ringo Starr, Robert Louis Stevenson, Fred Rogers, and Nikola Tesla. And unlike these leaders, our youth will have experienced social distancing worldwide; they're "doing isolation together." Independence from peer pressure and groupthink may be emerging as kids see the limits of satisfaction that media can bring and start to appreciate the embodied presence of others. It will be a defining moment for them. We must encourage them to embrace this new identity forged in hardship.*[46]

The narrative they develop, as in past generations, is in our hands.

Talk It Over

1. What are the greatest lessons we can learn from the Silent Generation?

2. How will we need to lead the Pandemic Population differently than we have so far?

3. How can you shape your students' story after looking at the Silent Generation?

THREE

What a Little Grit Can Accomplish During a Pandemic

In the early parts of 2020, I heard several people on television imply that the Spanish flu of 1918 was the last pandemic our world has seen.

But that's not true.

The truth is, our world endured a global outbreak between 1968 and 1970, when I was about nine years old. It was H3N2, or more commonly called the Hong Kong flu, and was very similar to COVID-19. It was actually the third pandemic of the twentieth century, following the 1918 Spanish flu and the 1957 influenza pandemic. This forgotten pandemic moved from nation to nation, eventually taking over a million lives. In fact, the CDC estimates between 1 and 4 million people died from it. In America, we experienced two waves: the first one ended early March 1969, and the second didn't flare up again until November of that year. By December 1969, it had arrived in all fifty states. (As US soldiers returned home from Vietnam, many brought the virus with them.) And right in the middle of that time period (August 1969) was Woodstock, the gigantic rock festival in Bethel, New York, where some 400,000 fans attended the four-day concert. In other words, while the virus was still active and we had no known cure, almost half a million people decided to camp together in the woods. I'm guessing there wasn't a lot of social distancing going on.

Sound a little different than today?

WHAT WAS SIMILAR IN THE TWO PANDEMICS

Before we talk about America's different response, let's talk about the similarities between H3N2 and COVID-19, which occurred about fifty years later.

Both viruses spread quickly, with symptoms of fever, cough, upper respiratory problems, and shortness of breath. For both viruses, the most vulnerable to infection were adults over sixty-five with underlying medical conditions, but both viruses could strike people of any age.

In fact, both H3N2 and COVID-19 did not spare the rich and famous, according to the New York Post. Both Tallulah Bankhead (a movie actress) and Allen Dulles (former CIA director) died of the Hong Kong flu. President Lyndon B. Johnson and Vice President Hubert Humphrey both fell ill from it and recovered, just as UK Prime Minister Boris Johnson grew ill with COVID-19 and recovered.

Both viruses ended up infecting animals, and both affected NASA astronauts. And during both pandemics, there were horror stories: while today we hear of bodies stored in refrigerator trucks in New York, during the 1969 H3N2 virus, corpses were stored in subway tunnels in Germany.

Our world took the Hong Kong flu in stride, with very little fanfare, which is why so few even remember it today. The *New York Post* notes that the New York Times called it "one of the worst in the nation's history,"[47] but our world didn't shut down. While it was a story on the news, it did not get lots of coverage on TV or front page headlines in newspapers. Schools didn't close, except for a few dozen because too many teachers were sick. Face masks were rarely worn. There was no run on toilet paper. When you consider the differences between then and now, this drastic different response is not that surprising. The virus was not handled by politicians but handled by doctors and communities with common sense. It was a different generation; leaders then approached viruses with calm rationality. We knew it was going on, but people were not paralyzed by it. My question is, Why? Should we have stopped everything like we've done today? Should we have grown paranoid over it like millions have done today? And if we had, would it have helped or hindered society?

How Life Is Different Today

Certainly, we've made great progress over the last fifty years in medicine and technology. I am grateful we can hear from medical experts on television who offer practical guidance to us for preventing the spread of the coronavirus. As a type one diabetic in my sixties, I value taking steps to stay healthy and strong during this outbreak today. What did our mothers used to say? "Better safe than sorry," right?

I have witnessed other changes, however, that have worsened our response today.

Due to both the 24-7 news cycle and the fear narrative most possess today, millions of adults have become paranoid about this virus. Certainly, our awareness has enhanced our willingness to obey orders that would have never flown in 1969. For example, other than washing hands and staying home when sick, few other precautions were taken during the Hong Kong flu. It is likely that if some of the precautions that are being taken now were taken during the Hong Kong flu, the death toll would have been much lower.

So, what happened that has so changed our response to a pandemic?

Jim Poling Sr. authored a book on the subject called, *Killer Flu: The World on the Brink of a Pandemic*. Jim actually caught the Hong Kong flu and survived. He says that much of our current thinking about infectious diseases in the modern era changed because of the SARS outbreak in 2003. He says, "It scared many people. It's the first time I recall people wearing masks and trying to distance themselves from others."[48]

"The idea that a pandemic could be controlled with social distancing and public lockdowns is a relatively new one," said Jeffrey Tucker, editorial director for the American Institute for Economic Research. The idea was first suggested in a 2006 study by New Mexico scientist Robert J. Glass. Interestingly, Glass got the idea from his 14-year-old daughter's science project. Utilizing Glass' recommendations, two government doctors (not even epidemiologists),Richard Hatchett and Carter Mecher, hatched the idea of using government-enforced social distancing and made plans to try it out on the next virus. "We are, in effect,"Tucker says,"part of a grand social experiment."[49]

The reality of social distancing is that it's an idea that probably wouldn't have caught on fifty years ago. At this time in our culture's history, however, we've developed a narrative of worry. I'm not saying taking precautions is senseless, but *worry* more than *wisdom* now dominates many parent's thinking.

- We worry our kids won't be safe.
- We worry we haven't done enough.
- We worry someone might file a lawsuit.
- We worry our child's self-esteem is fragile.
- We worry our kids won't get into the right college.
- We worry our children might catch COVID-19 outside.
- And now, we worry they won't have that great career awaiting them.

This "worry posture" has coerced us to change our very definition of common sense. Our amygdalae are on red alert (inside our brains), causing us not only to err on the side of caution but also to mitigate risks in a way that may hinder our kids' growth. We're in fight or flight mode far too often. And now, avoiding risk is the number one priority.

But there is always a trade off when we choose worry over wisdom.

In our work with thousands of schools, I've observed that our population is far more fragile than it was when I was growing up. I remember the Honk Kong flu—I turned ten years old in the fall of 1969. As I watched for cues for how to respond to it, however, I saw no one panicking. All of the caring adults in my life (parents, teachers, coaches, and employers) wanted to build kids that were tough and ready for adulthood when it was time. In fact, as Tucker reminded me, we were taught in "the '60s that getting viruses ultimately strengthened one's immune system. One of my most vivid memories is of a chickenpox party. The idea was that you should get it and get it over with when you are young."[50]

Our leaders took setbacks in stride, knowing they happen to everyone and the best response is to get stronger from them, not resentful toward them. Leaders were different. I remember the leaders in my life—my parents, teachers, and coaches—had a different view of. Here are just a few of the ways we viewed life differently back then:

A Different View of Safety

Like today, every parent wanted their child to be safe back then. My parents took measures to make me wear a seatbelt (when those were new) and to be wise when I played outside. Yet our view of safety was different. Trial and error was viewed as a great teacher. As a teen, I was in a bicycle accident going down a steep hill that cut me up so badly you could see my muscles under the skin just below my ribs. Watching my mom respond, however, shaped my worldview. She never panicked as she tended to my wounds. She empathized with my pain but stayed calm. And she didn't forbid me from riding a bike again to keep me safe. She and I talked about how I could be wiser when I rode it. Today, while I want my kids to be safe, I can't help but believe that our culture's view of safety has backfired. In our hypervigilance over safety, parents fear allowing their children to take part in activities that they commonly did unsupervised as a kids. In the same way, schools fear letting children and teens engage in activities that actually build grit and mature deci-sion-making skills, for fear of litigation.

A Higher Expectation of Resilience

As a child, resilience was an expected norm for everyone, including children. I was led by compassionate adults, but they never assumed I couldn't recover from hardship. I now count that as one of my most precious memories—my leaders actually believed in me and expected the best of me. As a young adult, I was involved in numerous car crashes (five in all). After ensuring I was okay, those same adults discussed with me how to handle myself in challenging driving situations and even challenged me to consider what I'd learned. I was able to laugh about those experiences later because of how well I was led through them. As a college student, I contracted type one diabetes and was given twenty years to live. (That was the average lifespan of a diabetic in 1980.) Those who treated me spoke to me as a young man who could learn a new way to live and, ultimately, outlive that prognosis—and I have. Early on, I wondered about my own capacity for resilience, but I bought into the narrative of my parents, doctors, nurses, and teachers. They expected resilience, and I met those expectations.

A Longer-term Perspective

As a child, I was conditioned to think long term. Life was about taking the curve balls you were thrown and making the most of them. Making lemonade out of lemons. As a young professional, I was traveling in New Zealand and was involved in a small plane crash. There were four of us on board and in our attempt to land on a field, our engine stalled and we dropped 120 feet to the ground. It was terrifying. I never blacked out. I was beaten up pretty badly and wore bandages on my ankle, ribs, and head for a while. I still have a mark on my ankle to this day. Needless to say, it was scary to hop back on a plane afterward, but I had to in order to return home. In fact, it was the best thing I could do: get back on the horse (or in this case, plane) and ride again. Any turbulence brought back vivid memories of the crash. Yet it forced me to grow, to learn from it all and take the long view. I had too much to accomplish, and I was still young. Today, I hop on 140 flights a year.

So, what can we learn from the past generation of leaders during the last pandemic?

BUILDING STRONG ADULTS FROM TODAY'S KIDS

There are clear lessons we can learn from the past, both good and bad ones. I offer three good ones below that we must recapture today. In chapter 1, I referred to the term *snowflake*. Let's examine some steps we can take to correct any leadership we've offered that cultivated a snowflake mindset and then let's examine steps we can take to prepare them to be the leaders they are capable of becoming.

Building Snowmen (and Women) from Snowflakes

1. Grit and Gravity

Zero-gravity environments cause muscles to atrophy. We learned this from NASA over fifty years ago. Astronauts in space had to perform exercises to prevent them from becoming weak in a space capsule that had no push or pull from gravity.

Metaphorically speaking, this principle is applicable on earth as well. When adults remove the "gravity" (the push or pull that stretches people), our young will be unable to do tasks that past generations of young adults were able to do. Strength comes with stretching. Grit grows with gravity. As their leaders, we must introduce (or allow) gravity to take effect, knowing it's a positive and essential element of their growth. Learning to pay bills, assuming responsibility for tasks, and negotiating projects with both teachers and employers cannot be learned on a screen or with a lecture. Learning these tasks require action. Growing up works like riding a bike. You must do it yourself. Sure, kids begin with a tricycle and then move on to a bike with training wheels. But eventually, the training wheels must come off, or embarrassment will prevail. Like teaching a child to ride a bike, our leadership must offer a balance between *support* and *letting go*.

Today, our young will only cultivate grit when they are forced to be resourceful. Grit comes, psychologist Angela Duckworth says, when students must reach down and find a way to achieve something on their own.[51] The more resources we give them, the less resourceful they tend to become. Further, research tells us we must encourage them to stick with a commitment for at least two years to see lasting results. So, when you hear a young person complain about how tough something is, just ask yourself, *Is my response or solution going to increase or decrease their grit?*

2. Control and Hope

In experiments with adolescent rats, psychologists discovered what they later called, "learned helplessness." It happens when a participant pursues a goal and when nothing happens for a period of time, they conclude the goal is out of their control. And they stop trying. In the study, rats stopped pulling a lever to get food when nothing happened.[52] Too often, our young give up due to "learned helplessness." This occurs, however in both a surprising and sinister fashion. It's all about control. Studies reveal that when the activities in their day are controlled by adults (and hence, not in their control), both their angst and hopelessness rise. The more we govern and prescribe the agenda, the less they feel hopeful and the more they feel helpless.

Further, learned helplessness promotes irresponsibility. Kids feel little responsibility to work because it's "not up to them." I believe most middle-class students assume that if they make a mistake, some adult will swoop in and rescue them. While this may feel like a good idea to parents, it actually hinders development. When kids feel that outcomes are in their control—even if it ultimately leads them to failure—it gives them a greater sense of hope and ownership.

Established generations must slowly encourage and even insist on giving Generation Z control of the "agenda." This is the only way to build ownership, engagement, and responsibility. It requires trust and flexibility, since young people may not perform to our standards. Ask yourself what you want most from them—perfection or growth?

3. Belief and Reality

What message do you suppose is sent to students when the adults in their lives continue to swoop in and save them whenever something goes wrong? While it may feel good at first, it communicates, "We don't think you have it in you to solve this problem. You need an adult to help you." Consequently, these young people don't feel like adults themselves until somewhere between ages twenty-six and twenty-nine. They can remain on their parents' insurance policy until age twenty-six. Julie Beck, senior editor at *The Atlantic*, conducted a survey and noted, "Of the responses readers sent in about their adult transitions, the most common answer was 'When I had children,'"—referring to when they felt like an adult.[53] Today, this doesn't happen until long after eighteen years old. So, while we give them the right to vote at eighteen, they may have no concept of "real life" until far later. Rights without responsibilities creates virtual adults and, far too often, spoiled brats.

As I mentioned earlier, adults have filled our kids' lives with artificial experiences. Their lives are like the real thing, but we've not trusted them to take on something genuinely important that has high stakes. And they've gotten the message loud and clear: You are just a child. You don't know better. You need help. You're not an adult.

Consider with me the impact and benefits of a different style of leadership. When an adult is both *supportive* and *demanding*, it accomplishes something amazing. The recipient of this style of leadership begins to believe in themselves, because their leader believed in them first. Instead of communicating "You need me," we instead communicate, "You've got this!" This belief-style leadership is best displayed when we offer real-life experiences to the young person. It may be an overseas trip or a job or even raising funds for a significant cause. Whatever it is, it's ultimately about setting great expectations. One experiment found that a specific type of feedback given to young teens increased the students' efforts between 40 and 300 percent. What was the feedback? It was simply "I'm giving you these comments because I have very high expectations and I know that you can reach them."[54] So, the next time you owe some feedback to a young person, ask yourself, *Are the remarks I am about to make communicating belief in them?*

TALK IT OVER

1. How does your leadership of young people either induce or reduce grit?

2. How does going on with normal life both help and hinder during a pandemic?

3. What specific steps could you take as you learn from leaders during the Hong Kong flu?

FOUR

A Pandemic Is a Terrible Thing to Waste

Many people I know complained about the "interruption" of the coronavirus when it first broke out. Life was put on hold. Classes went virtual or went away. For some, work stopped. It still feels like we're not making progress.

But really, whether or not we make progress is totally up to us.

I don't mean to sound flippant about this pandemic when many faced self-quarantines and even infections. I just believe that if we handle this interruption well, we might be surprised by what can be accomplished that would never have happened in our normal, busy routines.

Did you know that Isaac Newton was a college student during the Great Plague of London in 1665? Although it would take another two hundred years before doctors knew what caused it, folks had enough sense to send the students home to practice 'social distancing.'

And that's when the magic happened.

Cambridge sent students home, so Newton returned to Woolsthorpe Manor, the family estate about sixty miles northwest of campus. Without his teachers to guide him, Newton flourished. The year he spent away was later referred to as his *annus mirabilis*, the "year of wonders."[55]

First of all, he continued working on math problems on his own that he'd begun at Cambridge University. Believe it or not, the papers he wrote became the creation of calculus.

Second, he acquired some prisms and began experimenting with them in his room, even boring a hole in his shutters so only a small beam of light could shine through. From his explorations emerged his theories on optics.

Third, outside his window was an apple tree. Yes, the apple tree we've all heard about. While parts of the narrative are urban legend, his assistant confirmed much of it is true. While he was sitting under that tree, an apple fell which launched his thinking. *The same power of gravity which made an apple fall to the ground, he might have thought, was not limited to a certain distance from the earth (to a tree) but must extend much farther than was usually thought. "Why not as high as the moon?"...*

From this apple, Newton developed his theory on the law of gravity and laws of motion. Not bad progress for someone in quarantine.

WHAT WE LEARN FROM ISAAC NEWTON

Back in London, a fourth of the population would die of the plague between 1665 and 1666. It was one of many outbreaks during the four hundred years that the Black Plague ravaged Europe.[56]

Despite the terrible cost, because of Newton's efforts, we've all benefited from that outbreak.

Isaac Newton returned to Cambridge in 1667, with his theories in hand. Within six months, he was made a fellow. Two years later, he became a professor. Not bad for a young man.

So, what could we do during this time of social distancing? How could we encourage the Pandemic Population to see this moment in history as a time of possibility instead of loss?

Pandemics: An Interruption or an Introduction?

The concept I am introducing here is so simple that it eludes us. It was actually because Isaac Newton couldn't stay busy with his normal work that he made some of his most important discoveries. A big *interruption* became a big *introduction* to new discoveries and advantages. But he had to choose to make his problem a possibility, to make his obstacles opportunities. He had to invest his time, not waste it. The stumbling block to his education…became a stepping-stone for new learning.

So, how did he turn quarantine in his favor?

1. He had time and solitude to muse and to create.

I think most people run from solitude. We are conditioned to put our earplugs in and make noise. Turn the radio on. Drown out the boredom. While there's nothing wrong with this, it frequently prevents original thinking. Neuroscientists tell us that it's during times of boredom that our brains develop empathy and creativity. Fortunately, Isaac Newton had no video games or television in which to squander time. When nothing and no one consumed his time, he had time to imagine and come up with some timeless ideas.

2. He had ownership of his day to pursue what interested him.

When no one is around to tell us what to do, we ought to experience our greatest moments. We own those moments. Isaac Newton pursued the things he wanted when he wanted. He didn't squander his freedom. I'm sure he took time for fun, but his tasks were fun because he was in charge of them. Some call it "metacognition." Ownership creates initiative. Good things can happen when we have autonomy—we can master a passion.

3. He had margin to observe and to experiment.

A student's life in the twenty-first century is often full. A combination of classes, clubs, studies and sports leaves little margin in the week. Newton's life came to a halt just like yours and mine during the pandemic. He leveraged his days experimenting with light, exploring math equations, and writing new theories about how the world works. And it paid off. With brain bandwidth to observe and investigate, he was promoted twice in three years.

Today, I am so grateful Isaac Newton had some spare time. What will we do with ours?

FINDING OR EVEN CREATING A SILVER LINING

They key is going to be how we choose to look at this whole thing. And, as I have mentioned, the narrative we choose to tell ourselves once life returns to a new normal. The narrative we embrace, of course, will be derived from our perspective. How do we even perceive what's happening to us? Are we mere victims of a horrible time in history? Or could this be an opportunity for us to progress to a far better place? Once again, I pose the question, Is COVID-19 an interruption or an introduction to something better?

Although I usually hate interruptions in my week, I have learned they are often a segue into opportunity. Interruptions have a way of changing us and challenging us. We enter our week with a plan, and then suddenly, intrusions happen. People walk in with unsolicited problems. Accidents occur that require time and energy to fix. Outbreaks unexpectedly sweep across the world.

The Positive Outcomes of Outbreaks Through History

Because unplanned interruptions have a way of forcing people to be adaptable and resourceful, positive outcomes have often resulted from many of the outbreaks throughout history.

The Antonine Plague (165–180)

Many historians believe this epidemic was first brought to the Roman Empire by soldiers returning home after a war against Parthia. The epidemic contributed to a major shake-up of the established powers during that period:

- It forced the end of the Pax Romana (the Roman Peace), a period from 27 BC to AD 180, when Rome colonized and dominated much of the world.

- Afterward, instability grew throughout the Roman Empire, leading to civil wars and invasions by "barbarian" groups.[57]

- People began to reflect and prioritize personal and spiritual matters over materialism. Family and faith became increasingly popular after the plague occurred.

Not bad for an outbreak.

The Black Death (1346–1353)

Mass graves were dug to bury the dead in this horrible plague that traveled from Asia to Europe. Some historians believe it wiped out half of Europe's population. The plague changed the course of Europe's history and brought these benefits:

- With so many dead, labor became harder to find, bringing about better pay for workers and the end of Europe's system of serfdom.
- Surviving workers had better access to meat and higher-quality bread, and afterward lived longer lives.[58]
- The lack of cheap labor may also have contributed to technological innovation. With fewer workers, people had to get creative to maintain output.

Not bad for an outbreak.

The American Polio Epidemic (1916)

My parents told me about polio, the deadly and disparaging disease that prevailed as they grew up. Franklin D. Roosevelt contracted it at thirty-nine years old. Polio had existed for a long time, but it often takes an *outbreak* before we get a *breakthrough*:

- As Americans watched FDR, their president, battle this disease, it became top of mind for millions of citizens.
- As polio became an epidemic, it drove urgency for the discovery of a vaccine, which was finally created by Jonas Salk in 1954.
- Worldwide vaccination efforts now take place to reduce and eradicate the disease.

Not bad for an outbreak.

So, with all the negative outcomes we see from today's coronavirus, what if we looked it at differently. Whenever I see a problem, I tell myself, *I can get mad or I can get busy.*

These past epidemics may just show us how to get busy:

- What if we let the adversity weed out what's wrong and clarify what's important?
- What if we let the adversity catalyze wise decisions to improve conditions?
- What if we let the adversity create an urgency about solving your biggest problems?

There's almost always some good that can stem from adverse situations. It just requires us and the young people we lead to think big picture and long term and take the high road.

What good can you already see coming as a result of the coronavirus?

How to Turn a Setback into a Comeback

I want to tell you a story that has a relevant application to this season we're in today. If you know anything about professional boxing history over the last century, you know the name Jack Dempsey. Jack was the heavyweight champion of the world for seven years.

But do you know the name of the guy who finally beat him?

Probably not. He was a nobody by the name of Gene Tunney. Gene had set a goal as a young man that he wanted to be a professional boxer—until he faced a setback during his military service when Gene broke all of the fingers in both of his hands. His trainer and his doctor both told him he'd have to give up boxing. His brittle bones would not allow it.

Gene had a decision in front of him.

Interestingly, Gene decided he would not give up his goal to be a boxer. In fact, he wanted to be the heavyweight champion of the world. He'd just change his methods to get ready. Gene began to learn the art of self-defense, which allowed him to use a different part of his hand for his craft. He learned to move backward, knowing that to beat Jack Dempsey he'd have to move backwards for a few rounds. In other words, his injury didn't change his goal, it just completely changed the way he approached his goal.

When Gene Tunney finally got his chance to take on Jack Dempsey, Gene whipped Jack. It shocked everyone. It so humiliated Jack Dempsey, that He challenged Gene to a rematch. Gene beat him a second time. He was no fluke.

Now, here's the truth I want you to catch. Fistic experts, who understand boxing, tell us something intriguing. They estimate there is no way that Gene Tunney could have beaten Jack Dempsey for the heavyweight crown had he not broken all the fingers in both of his hands. No one at the time could go head to head and toe to toe with Dempsey and survive. The very setback (even tragedy) Gene faced actually launched him toward the goal.

His *setback* actually enabled him to *come back* better.

What We Learn from Gene Tunney

Gene practiced three responses that empowered him to go further than he expected when he faced a setback. These three practices leveraged his injury and propelled him toward his original goal:

> **Continue**: First, he decided to not give up on his original goal. He continued pushing forward.

> **Adapt**: Next he adapted how he'd chase his goal. He kept his mission but changed his methods.

> **Reverse**: The he took the very problem that could've shut him down and used it to send him on.

I'm not sure how the adverse circumstances of this season have felt like a setback for you or the Generation Z students you lead. Whatever it's looked like for you, my challenge for you is this: What if you took the very challenge you saw as a disadvantage and reversed it, making it an advantage? What if this time-out during the coronavirus could be leveraged to move you and your students further faster?

Developing Resilience

Author Jim Collins introduced us to the "Stockdale Paradox." Admiral Jim Stockdale was a prisoner of war (POW) during the Vietnam War. He talks about the power of hope, that enabled him to endure the atrocities of torture and death all around him. He said, "I never lost faith in the end of the story. I never doubted not only that I would get out, but also that I would prevail in the end and turn the experience into the defining event of my life, which, in retrospect, I would not trade."[59]

When Collins asked Stockdale about the POWs who were mostly likely not make it out of Vietnam, Stockdale replied, "The optimists. Yes. They were the ones who always said, 'We're going to be out by

Christmas.' Christmas would come and it would go. And there would be another Christmas. And they died of a broken heart."[60]

Stockdale's insight can teach us a very important lesson. You must never confuse faith that you will prevail in the end, which you can never afford to lose, with the discipline to confront the most brutal facts of your current reality, whatever they might be.

The Stockdale Paradox is a paradox indeed. It's all about confronting the harsh realities of your current setbacks—not denying them—but also relentlessly holding on to the hope that you will one day prevail. It's not merely being an optimist. It's about embracing unshakable faith.

This is where resilience comes in.

If the Pandemic Population will rise from the ashes of this health hazard and economic downturn, they will need to become practiced in the art of resilience. Loads of books and speakers bring up the necessity of resilience, but it's not much help unless we break down what that means. Resilience includes two chief ingredients:

Ambition: This is the strong aspiration, even resolve, to reach a goal. No one bounces back from a setback unless they really want to. With a strong enough ambition, determination kicks in. I believe we must look for any hints of ambition and resolve in these Generation Z kids and fan it into flame.

Adaptability: This is the capacity to flex and modify the original approach to stay on course. No one bounces back from a setback unless they're willing to switch game plans in light of the goal. I believe we need to condition Generation Z kids to hold their goals or aspirations more sacred than their methods or plans.

Consider the Great Depression kids we examined in chapter two. Adults in their life fanned into flame their ambitions, and kids assumed they'd need that ambition if they had any hope of making it. If you recall, many said they didn't even know they were in a "Great Depression" because it was just what life was like in that time period. They weren't victims. Few that I spoke to even compared themselves to someone else. They just pursued their goals.

In 1932, Charles Darrow had lost much of what he'd worked for as a salesman during the early years of the Great Depression. He and his wife were tempted to give up but decided to find a way to 'monetize' their hopes by creating an activity they played together after supper. They dreamed of becoming millionaires and began discussing what they would do if they had a million dollars. Next they added play money, and then they added houses and hotels and a gameboard. That same year, the game was complete. Charles had invented a game that you likely have in your house today: Monopoly. In 1935, Parker Brothers bought the game from him and fulfilled his dreams. They gave him a million dollars for the rights to the game.[61]

In 1931, Alfred Butts lived in New England with no job and no prospects for work. He and many of his friends fought their despair by escaping reality. After hours of futile job hunting, Alfred would sit down on the porch of a storefront in town to kill time. He noticed a growing number of people biding their time doing crossword puzzles. He decided he'd try to monetize their love of that activity and ended up creating the game of Scrabble. He made a great living off of an invention that began in the midst of the Great Depression.[62]

Both of these cases represent the positives that can emerge from hardship. Both men didn't focus on what they lacked, but they focused on what they loved. Instead of complaining, they started creating. They forced themselves to respond when faced with harsh realities. What began as survival became success. This is what resilience could do for this young generation too as long as we lead them correctly.

I say, a pandemic is a terrible thing to waste.

TALK IT OVER

1. How could you and your students "weed out what's wrong and clarify what's important" following the coronavirus quarantine?

2. What is one setback you've experienced? How could it become a comeback for you?

3. What essential steps should you take to remain hopeful without falling into the superficial trap of uninformed optimism?

FIVE

The Positive and Negative Impacts of COVID-19 on Today's Youth

I read three authors who recently compared our pandemic experience to a new weather pattern. They described it as harsh weather that we will have to learn to endure and safeguard ourselves from for quite some time. One of the authors, a social scientist, believed it is most helpful to describe our "new normal" as follows:[63]

We are now facing a blizzard.

The quarantine lasted for months and its outcomes will continue to annoy most of us. It was like being hit with very bad weather that shut us all inside our homes. We watched and heard about victims of the coronavirus on television.

It is part of a longer winter season.

The new normal we've entered will likely last a year to a year and a half (or more). Beginning in March 2020, we began to hear doctors, scientists, and celebrities talk about bracing for a longer-term pattern that will force us to get used to a new lifestyle.

Which is all part of a new ice age.

Winter, of course, represents a shorter period of time than an era or "ice age." We're not certain about the specifics, but we may be entering a new era for the next four to six years. We may interact differently, handle work differently, shop differently, and live differently.

As we learned earlier from Admiral Jim Stockdale, the key will be to embrace the Stockdale Paradox. We must face reality, no matter how harsh it seems, but never lose hope that we will beat this thing in the end. We must not use "optimistic" language like "It will all be over by next month!" Instead, we must use language like "In the end, we will find a way to thrive in our new reality and reach our potential.

This is why we must be intentional.

How the Coronavirus Could Affect Us All…Especially Generation Z

As I pointed out earlier, every time period in history is shaped by the significant events that occur during that season. Each generation is marked by shared experiences, music, heroes, villains, tragedies, and TV shows.

Today's generation will undoubtedly be deeply affected by this health emergency we now call the coronavirus (COVID-19) pandemic. Globally, nations took steps to keep people safe. College and professional sports competitions were put on hold. People wore masks when commuting. Shoppers hoarded toilet paper and hand sanitizer. Employees worked virtually from home and most everyone began canceling social and business meetings, choosing to meet more safely on a screen. We even witnessed national lockdowns. And most surprising of all, it all happened so fast—changing our reality in just a matter of weeks.

In 2020, I heard more than one person say, "What a crazy year last week has been."

The Negative and Positive Impact of the Season We Are Living In

The fact is, we may see some habits begin that stay with us for years. Like the aftershock of an earthquake, mindsets and lifestyles will likely form during this season that spread throughout the world and continue long after COVID-19 is history. We may travel differently and work differently for years to come. Time will tell how the pandemic genuinely affects us, but I predict we may see Generation Z growing up in a "new normal" just like millennials did following September 11, 2001. Let's look at some of the effects—both positive and negative—that could remain in the Pandemic Population.

Three Potential Negative Effects

1. The normalization of isolation.

While life will eventually return to some version of normal, I believe teleworking will likely be here to stay. Working remotely is already happening in businesses across the country—and employers are learning how much can get done virtually from home. Employees are learning it's more convenient and cost-effective to stay home. What we'll lack is needed face-to-face connections. Humans are social creatures that require time together. We've already learned screens are not enough to meet our social needs. Sadly, society migrates toward convenience whenever possible, even if it costs us our mental and emotional health.

2. The normalization of panic and anxiety.

Our culture has already witnessed the rise in anxiety, depression, and mental health problems. I believe our reaction to COVID-19 will deepen the normalization of panic. When I review Americans' reaction to the influenza, swine flu, and SARS outbreaks of the past, society was far less fragile emotionally. The reproductive rate (r0) of the coronavirus is less than SARS, smallpox, or the mumps. Ebola had a fatality rate of half of those infected, far higher than COVID-19. Certainly, we must take action—but panic usually worsens things. We must fight anxiety like we fight the coronavirus.

3. The normalization of a scarcity mindset.

Since the year 2000, our culture has experienced two economic downturns—and our current pandemic may just cause a third one. Far worse than sour economies, however, is the scarcity mindset that can accompany difficult times: "It feels like things are running out; like there won't be enough of what we need." The Great Depression of 1929 wasn't the result of a stock market crash alone. It was also caused by panicked people who rushed to the banks to withdraw money, further ensuring the banks would collapse. We must work to ensure the coronavirus doesn't remove hope, faith, and optimism from Generation Z.

Three Potential Positive Effects

1. The expansion of resourcefulness and innovation.

Just like difficult times encouraged frugality in my parent's generation during the 1930s, this season could foster resourcefulness and innovation in Generation Z. Since we often get creative when routines are on hold, some will figure out how to monetize our new normal. Kids could become more creative with their smart devices and find a way to capitalize on hardship. Jacob Schick invented an electric razor when he cut himself shaving. Charles Kettering got the idea for an electronic ignition when he broke his arm starting a car. When resources are scarce, well-led kids become resourceful.

2. The expansion of saving and giving.

I love our societal predisposition toward "paying it forward." It's common to hear stories of people paying off another person's medical bills or the food for the car behind them at a drive-through window. I'm hopeful this pandemic conditions students to see how they can serve others or give to those less fortunate. I'm also hopeful this season encourages students to save money instead of spending it or wasting it. I'm hopeful this pandemic teaches us to think about the future, not just today, and think of others, not just ourselves.

3. The expansion of responsive service workers.

After 9/11, there were many young adults who believed our country needed heroes and enlisted in the military or decided to become first responders. While I realize this is an "apples and oranges" comparison, the coronavirus pandemic might have a similar effect. Generation Z members may recognize the need for nurses and emergency workers and respond. They will likely see the merit of medical professionals and the need for research. Both witnessing the need and the heroes who meet such needs can be a compelling argument to challenge a new workforce entering adulthood.

It's too early to be certain what the Pandemic Population will do with this strange period during their childhood. There will likely be both positive and negative outcomes. What we do know for sure is this: seldom does a generation experience such a dramatic collective experience without being shaped by it.

Which of these potential negative and positive outcomes do you see?

In the next chapter, we will dive into some ideas for leading the Pandemic Population into a better "new normal." The key to our leadership will be intentionality. We must not sit back and wait for something to happen. Instead we must choose to foster the positive and redemptive paradigms inside of them.

GAP YEAR VS. GRIPE YEAR

As COVID-19 tightened its grip around our teens and young adults laying plans for post- graduation, a growing number of them have considered taking a "gap year." This means, instead of taking the traditional route of enrolling in a four-year liberal arts college, graduate school, or even going on to work, they are taking time away to reflect and to grow.

It makes sense, doesn't it?

With colleges admitting they're not sure what classes will look like (at least in the near future) and with many schools migrating online (digital that which they may or may not host as well as in-person courses), students are wondering why they should spend all that tuition money on a risk. According to *The Chronicle of Higher Education*, "One in six high-school seniors who expected to attend a four-year college full time before the outbreak of the novel coronavirus now think that they will choose a different path this fall."[64]

Both of my kids took a gap year and consider it the smartest post-secondary decision they made. They both worked as interns and learned to serve a mission, to talk to customers on the phone, to travel and make a sale, to plan strategy, and to do the hard work that is often given to interns. It was the best way to prepare them for what was next, which for both of them was a university. When they enrolled, they were genuinely ready with the life skills, not just the intellect, they would need. Intentionality was paramount.

But if we're not intentional to help teens lay plans like these, this season could become a gripe year. You see, it is just as easy for students to note the uncertainties of our current educational world, and just do nothing but complain about it all. Instead of *seizing the moment* to do something different and prepare themselves, they may *size up the moment* and gripe about it all.

The rest of this book is about challenging the Pandemic Population to lead the way and committing ourselves to serve as guides on their journey. Choices lie ahead. We must acknowledge, however, that Generation Z, and specifically the Pandemic Population, look at life and change and leadership differently than their parents, teachers, coaches, and employers. They can emerge brilliantly from this period, but still turn out differently than we'd expect them to. We may just have to learn to accept this truth.

How Student Leadership Is Morphing for Generation Z

Before the COVID-19 outbreak, our young had begun to form a different view of how our world would change and should change.

"I see leadership differently than my parent's generation does."

Those are the words of Brandon, a college sophomore, who ended his semester at home, when the entire student body at Vanderbilt University left campus due to COVID-19. The coronavirus is changing us, and Brandon believes it is only accelerating a change that was taking place already.

In those days, I hosted a virtual meeting with students, ages seventeen to twenty-two, the ones I now call a "Pandemic Population." Just as they were making major decisions about their future, prom, graduation speeches, and careers, everything got put on hold. In times like these, people tend to reflect more about life, people, and their beliefs. Here are these students' responses to my questions about being a leader today.

1. **How do you see leadership differently than older generations?**

   I think my parents' and grandparents' generation sees leadership as a position to fill and a responsibility to fulfill. I see it as activism. Even millennials colored within the lines when they were students on campus. We feel leadership is about making changes to corruption, waste, misspending, and the mistreatment of marginalized people.

2. Is your activism like past activism in the 1960s?

There are some similarities. Fifty-plus years ago, people marched and demonstrated for equal rights and against corruption. Some call us neo-activists, and we are taking on those and other issues, like student-loan debt and immigration reform. One difference may be that neo-activists today pay homage to the past but are more intersectional in perspective. (Over half of students today who identify as an activist are involved in seven or more causes.)[65] We believe many issues intersect and reinforce each other. We see how #blacklivesmatter and #metoo overlap. There's greater solidarity.

3. So, do you not believe in serving in a formal leadership position?

No, it's not that. It's just that too often we see the position is merely a figurehead or the top job in a corrupt system. Position doesn't necessarily offer a voice. So, we would rather influence in more of a grassroots way. I'd rather influence my residence hall without being an RA.

4. Doesn't student leadership and activism hinder your academic experience?

I'm sure some teachers and parents are scared we are distracted from classes or are wasting our time. But our group chats seem to tell us there is no negative impact from our sit-ins, marches, and organized protests. In fact, those of us who are active are actually doing better in class because we are connecting theory and practice. It's helping us become stronger students and critical thinkers.

5. What do you wish educators would do to support your leadership?

We think most administrators see us as annoying. We're a painful disruption to the schedules they hold sacred. But we just want to be heard. We know we represent risk to how they appear to stake-holders in the community. It doesn't have to be that way. Maybe they could start by attending a club meeting or a gathering to listen to us.

6. When a college makes a change in response to activists, do you feel you've succeeded?

Yes, in a sense we do. Probably the classic example was when the University of Missouri mounted a huge protest against a racist campus culture. It began with eleven students and grew into thousands. It was called Concerned Student 1950. It resulted in the resignation of the university president and chancellor. We don't want violence. We don't want a we-they culture. We want things to get better and we feel that if we let the status quo remain, nothing will change. Many of our administrators were once college students who felt the gap between them and those in power. Now that they're in power, they do not seem to want change and just want to hold on to the power.

7. How do you think most from Generation Z choose to influence?

Two things come to mind. First, we know we are customers. Schools want our money (or our parent's money), so we take advantage of the fact that we can display the customer isn't happy. Second, we have a smart phone and know we can use social media to spread our message as fast as any generation. Maybe faster. We will use this as long as it gives the average person influence.

8. Is this the wave of the future?

I don't know. One day we'll grow older and who knows what new technology will appear. I do think we'll always need good leaders, whether or not they hold a position. I think generational change comes before social change. When we're older, I'll be curious to see if we carry these values with us into adulthood. I hope we do, and I hope it draws us all closer.

TALK IT OVER

1. Is there anything you can learn from this my interactions with Generation Z as you develop young influencers?

2. What do you anticipate will be a response from the Pandemic Population?

3. How could you encourage positive responses from the Pandemic Population?

Turning Post-Traumatic Stress into Post-Traumatic Growth

I just listened in on a discussion made up of students between the ages of seventeen and twenty-four years old. Overall, the conversation was positive, but it grew melancholy when we began to talk about the future. Usually, young men and women are optimistic and hopeful about what's coming after graduation. Not these students. They feel as if part of their life has been hijacked. Listen in:

> *"I can't get over this feeling of depression. All my plans following graduation are gone. The job I had lined up and my apartment and roommate plans have slipped through my fingers."*

> *"I'm going to miss saying goodbye to my friends in person, now that we're finishing the year from home. We won't have a graduation ceremony. No prom. No senior week. I know it's not a big deal in the grand scheme of things, but I feel that I am missing out on some milestones."*

> *"I feel I have to start all over, from scratch. It's like the stuff I accumulated on my transcripts and résumé don't matter as much because millions will be hunting for work we're done with this COVID-19 crisis. I cried last night for the first time in months."*

Life Inside a Parenthesis

Much like the kids of the Great Depression and World War II, there is a cohort of today's kids who are coming of age in a very different and difficult time. Life was progressing well for millions of them; the economy was good and prospects were hopeful. And then a pandemic occurred. A pandemic is an epidemic with a passport. It travels the world. In the case of this pandemic, it pushed pause on life as we know it—commerce, travel, education, entertainment, and jobs. And it has had a particular effect on those just coming of age. Who is this micro generation and what have they experienced? They are a subset of Generation Z. They're seventeen to twenty-two years old who feel delayed by COVID-19. Just as they were entering a new life station, life was postponed.

You could even call them a *Parenthetical Population*. By this I mean that they seem caught inside of a parenthesis in this moment. They are on hold. While it sounds strong, many of them feel

- postponed
- pushed aside
- penalized
- panicked

The teens in this group believe part of the typical American experience was lost to a pandemic. No prom. No signed yearbooks. No graduation ceremony. They feel grief. Loss. Angst. Isolation. These kids were caught in limbo and will require special leadership from us. Young professionals in this group need it just as much. "They're walking a tight rope and there are cliffs on either side," said Kathryn Edwards, a labor economist at the Rand Corporation. "It's hard to imagine someone making it through both of these recessions in this age group really unscathed."[66]

In many ways, this title is not even limited to a graduate today. Russ graduated from college in 2009, when the Great Recession was in full swing. He struggled to find work, and a decade later, he still struggles to find work that pays a decent wage. Russ is a young professional sandwiched between two economic declines. His mentors told him, "Dude, you missed the good times by like five years."

Bloomberg summarizes it this way: "Economic downturns are inevitable, but they're not usually so severe. And once-in-a-generation recessions don't tend to occur just a decade apart."[67] Think about the ramifications. Almost half of US households who are fifty-five and older have nothing saved for retirement.[68] In a new recession, millions of baby boomers will stay in their jobs longer because they can't retire. This means higher paying jobs are unavailable for the youngest population. In other words, this "parenthetical" moment Generation Z feels trapped in could go on for years.

Consider for a moment how different this crisis was compared to others in the past:

1. There was no official "start" to this calamity. It snuck up and ambushed us. There is no "remember where you were when…" conversation about COVID-19 like there was with 9/11. Our busy lives slowly came to a halt, and soon we found ourselves quarantined at home.

2. While it's national and global, it's also very local. The coronavirus spread from China to Europe to Washington state—and then all over the world. It infected people who live in 140 countries, yet the impact is uneven across them. The pain of this global virus feels personal.

3. For weeks, Americans got mixed messages about what the virus is, how contagious it is, how to avoid it, and how to treat it. First, we were told masks won't help, then we were told to wear masks. At first, we were told it wasn't airborne, then research came out that it can travel through air. At first, kids weren't vulnerable, and then they were.

4. We couldn't emote in group gatherings. Other crisis moments brought people together and created makeshift memorials. But COVID-19 forced us into isolation, unable to convene in ways we normally would. In fact, thousands died but family members had to stage virtual memorial services. Babies were born, and family members couldn't hold the newborn.

5. There was a diffusion of mortality. By April 2020, coronavirus cases in the United States were over one million; deaths surpassed 50,000. When a large group of people die in one specific location or a few locations (like during 9/11), we can get our heads around the grief and impact. But when mortality is diffused, it is harder to comprehend.

6. There is ambiguity and uncertainty about how bad it is and will be. Other moments of crisis seemed to have clearer boundaries. In this case, we don't have uniform acceptance of how big the problem is or what to do about it. That's why we had students on spring break saying, "It won't stop my partying" and one governor tweeting a selfie from a food court (on a weekend), saying, "Enjoy going out,"[69] while others are staying home.

7. There is absolute uncertainty about the future. After hosting a focus group of university students, I discovered how the ambiguity was holding them hostage mentally. Future plans had disappeared (at least temporarily), and having no plan deepened their stress levels. They admitted their whole life had been structured up till now—and suddenly it's completely unstructured and they're at home with no vision of what could happen.

A question I'm pondering is, How will these differences (and others) change the way the COVID-19 pandemic imprints this generation of students?

ANOTHER WALK DOWN MEMORY LANE

In his book *The Power of Bad*, author John Tierney reminds us of the power that tragic moments have over those who survive them:

> *Researchers are revising the traditional view of psychological trauma, which emerged after World War I when soldiers were diagnosed with the novel condition of "shell shock." Later called "Post-Vietnam syndrome," it was eventually known by the broader term post-traumatic stress disorder (PTSD). The disorder was quite real—and one more manifestation of the negativity effect. Some bad events, unlike good events, would affect people for decades or for life. When a bad event had permanent effects, like an accident that left someone unable to use their arms or legs, it could permanently reduce a person's level of happiness.[70]*

Interestingly, stress doesn't have to cause a disorder. It can also be leveraged for good. In his work, Tierney found that beginning in the 1990s, psychologists also noticed something else. At least half the population who endured a traumatic event showed no signs or symptoms of past-traumatic stress. Four out of five trauma victims did not suffer from PTSD afterward. In fact, typically they emerged even stronger. Instead of being permanently scarred by the tragedy, they experienced what is called post-traumatic growth (PTG). This term was introduced by psychologists Richard Tedeschi and Lawrence Calhoun. Some believe that it is not nearly as well-known as PTSD because good is never as newsworthy as bad. Even so, PTG is far more common. Studies reveal that more than 60 percent, and even as high as 90 percent, of trauma victims undergo post-traumatic growth, including ones who initially showed symptoms of PTSD.[71]

This realization has left me with a question: Is there a method to better guarantee that a person can walk away from traumatic events showing signs of PTG rather than PTSD?

Psychologists now use a chart to track PTG. These people experience

- increased appreciation of life
- deeper relationships with others
- new perspectives and priorities
- greater personal strength

The growth doesn't come from the trauma but from the way the person responds to it. These people suppress their negativity bias with an array of defenses that are available to anyone. They choose to become kinder, stronger, and more mindful of the joys in life. While a negative experience triggers a stronger immediate emotional reaction than a positive experience, negative emotions actually fade faster than positive ones do in most people. Repeated experiments with people who have undergone negative experiences prove this. They come into the lab and describe how they feel about recent events, and they later return to recall those same events. By then, their feelings have diminished, but the negative ones fade faster than the positive ones, especially among those who've repeatedly discussed the bad experience with others. Since the initial threat is over, they're prone to recognize the positive recovery that has taken place. In short, the more you talk about your problems, the more perspective you can gain to ease your anxieties. This is why we feel it is therapeutic to go to therapy.[72]

Within this truth is the answer to our question. We must pivot as we lead this Pandemic Population to make sure they experience growth, not stress, on the other side of the pandemic.

What's your biggest take away from John Tierney's ideas?

Steps to Turn PTSD into PTG

If the goal is to lead this Pandemic Generation away from PTSD and toward PTG, we may need to adapt the way we talk to them and lead them so they can change their internal narrative. In light of our current less-than-optimal realities, I suggest these steps:

1. **Acknowledge their disappointment and loss.**

   Have a conversation where you specifically address the elephant in the room: they have lost part of their growing-up experience. You might see it on their face. They may feel cheated, frustrated, or disappointed. Telling them it's not a big deal only discounts what they feel—making them feel worse. What they need is validation ("I know this is hard"), context ("Here is the need of the hour"), and belief ("We will get through this"). Just like a doctor uses a stethoscope on our hearts to diagnose us before she offers a treatment, we must show empathy first before we talk about a prescription for their sense of loss. Listen to their heart (What are they feeling?), look into their eyes (What have they seen?), ask about their ears (What have they heard?), and pay attention to their mouth (What have they said?).

2. **Stage an alternative rite of passage.**

   Proms were canceled. Graduation parties were canceled. Ceremonies were virtual at best. These important celebrations that say "Look at you! You are growing up! We are so proud of you!" were canceled, leaving kids with no closure. The few rites of passage we have in America vanished into thin air. So, what if you created some alternatives? For instance, during the quarantine, I saw large extended family/friends schedule a Google Hangout or Zoom call where each one expressed a single word that best described their affirmation for their Generation Z student. Others hosted a progressive dinner, where they drove from house to house allowing friends or family to chip in a dish or dessert to celebrate (at a distance). These creative alternatives could be the most memorable experience some students take from this global pandemic.

3. Include peer outsiders when you can.

Consider for a moment their friends—peers who were also in a shelter-in-place mandate. If they were quarantined in an unhealthy home and there was abuse, it may have only worsened. If they were in a passive home, their parents may be failing to shape the narrative they accumulate as they enter young adulthood. Could you find a way to invite peers who need intentional leadership temporarily into your fold and offer emotional support to them as well? You can keep the number small and still do some good. This could actually have a positive influence on both those kids and your kids. When we did this as our children grew up, it was always a positive. No one felt left out. Our own kids didn't feel slighted and everyone was loved and affirmed in times of challenge. The most powerful outcome you likely find is that when you include a friend or peer and he or she responds well to your input, it can have a positive peer-pressure effect on your own kids.

4. Enable them to turn their focus outward.

I have observed that anxiety feeds narcissism and narcissism feeds anxiety. When kids are focused on themselves, it only hastens poor mental health. Sadness sets in. They may never feel they're getting what they're entitled to receive. On the other hand, all of us gain a huge boost in our perspective when we learn to live for something bigger than us. Christine Carter, PhD, writes, "Again and again, research has shown that even in dire circumstances we feel better when we turn our attention to supporting others. This is true for teenagers, as well. It's not surprising that teens who provide tangible, emotional, or informational support to people in crises tend to feel more strongly connected to their community. They cope with their own challenges more effectively, and they feel more supported by others."[73]

5. Tell stories of heroes who overcame past tragedies.

I mentioned earlier, my dad was born in 1930, which meant the first decade of his life was marked by the Great Depression and the next five years were marked by World War II. He's told me those days were the best days of his life, not because they were easy but because people came together to help each other and to forge their way through a difficult time. Like today's COVID-19 pandemic, the economy spiraled down and unemployment was high. Hearing his stories always inspired me as a kid growing up. They were stories of the resilient and resourceful human spirit at its best. I suggest you find and share stories that could inform the narrative today's students should have. Some of the greatest discoveries and scientific advances have happened during and after epidemics, tragedies, and wars throughout history. People created new vaccines, designed new machinery, and even launched new industries because 'necessity is the mother of invention.'

6. Model the habit of finding a silver lining.

My mother, also a product of the Great Depression, did this spectacularly, without becoming corny or cliché. She naturally saw the blessing in disguise from almost any setback or hardship our family endured. When I got cut from the baseball team or got a less than stellar grade on a science project, she'd always grieve with me for a while but then inevitably she'd spot something positive that could come from the negative. When I was nine, I entered the kitchen for breakfast one morning, and we had only two choices for cereal. When she saw I was ready to grumble, she said, "Look at it this way, Timothy—our choice to make today is so much easier!" Her most potent influence on me in this regard, however, was when she naturally did this in her own experience. She spotted a silver lining in every dark cloud in her life, and her example conditioned me to grow up doing the same. It wasn't denial—she clearly faced her negative realities. It was simply her ability to see the good in every situation that made me a better person. In this way, my narrative was shaped by my mother's grateful, positive outlook.

7. Help them shape their internal narrative.

This may be the most important intentional step you can take. Research psychologist Brene Brown reminds us we are constantly telling a story to ourselves—about who we are and how we are doing.[74] It's an internal narrative that informs our confidence levels and the way we approach relationships, work, and life itself. This narrative begins during childhood. It's how our students develop their self-esteem and confidence. If we don't lead them well, our young people could unwittingly fall into a victim narrative:

- "Life is hard and it's not worth it."
- "I'll never get ahead."
- "I'm at a disadvantage."
- "I won't be able to reach my goals."

This story we tell ourselves informs how we think, how we feel about a situation, and even how we choose to act. Our internal narrative significantly influences what we experience in life—positively or negatively—regardless of whether it is accurate. It affects our happiness, our worry, and our level of satisfaction. It's been proven that the story we tell ourselves about the reality in front of us influences our lives as much as the reality itself.

This reality came to be known as the placebo effect and there is enormous scientific evidence about its effectiveness. Scientists like Irving Kirsch have shown remarkable effects from placebos. They are not only able to change the way we feel, they can actually have physical effects on our bodies. During World War II, we heard stories of medical doctors who ran out of opioid-based painkillers as they treated wounded soldiers. Anesthetist Henry Beecher was worried he'd give his soldier heart failure if he operated on them without numbing the area, so he tried an experiment. He told his patients he was giving them morphine, when in fact he was giving them nothing more than a saltwater drip. The patients reacted just as if they'd been given morphine. While we often look back at the discovery of the placebo effect with a smirk, we all know of many occasions when what we believe about something completely affects our reaction to it.[75] Authors Jonathan Haidt and Greg Lukianoff put it this way: "We are not saying that the problems facing students, and young people more generally, are minor or 'all in their heads.' We are saying that what people choose to do in their heads determines how those real problems affect them."[76]

Which of these strategies are you currently using? Which ones could be helpful to add?

SHAPING THEIR POST-PANDEMIC NARRATIVE

PTG is stimulated by choosing the narrative. Again from John Tierney's book, *The Power of Bad*, we find a few specific strategies drawn from his research into positive psychology. "Wounded soldiers and accident victims," for instance, "experience post-traumatic growth by rewriting the story of their lives. They see the injury not as something that shattered their plans but as something that started them on a new path. This same technique can be used for any kind of bad event in life. Being fired from a job can be seen not as a failure or a career killer, but as the impetus that leads to a better career."

Part of the reason for the success of these types of narrative shifts occurs because, as some psychologists have found, the power of sharing joy with others far outweighs the power of sharing grief. "Their term for [this] is capitalization. The psychologists Shelly Gable and Harry Reis have studied its effects by analyzing diaries and watching people in the laboratory talk about good things that have happened to them. When someone responds enthusiastically to your good news, you feel happier and the triumph seems more significant." In other words, "It takes two to capitalize on good news." As poet John Milton says, "Good, the more communicated, more abundant grows."

This can actually be an intentional practice you launch with a young person. You can set it up as you would practicing a sport by scheduling time to actively pursue the goal. It involves looking backward to the past to imagine a better future. Tierney recommends two specific ideas:

Firstly, try having your students list their "blessings. Cultivating an "attitude of gratitude" is one of the most effective strategies identified by the positive psychology movement." Just simply "write a list of five things for which you're grateful. It can be a specific event of the day or something general like "wonderful friends."

Secondly, another proven strategy you can have them try "is the 'gratitude visit': Write a three-hundred-word letter to someone who changed your life for the better, listing specific reasons, and then visit them and read it aloud."[77]

Steps like these are just a start, but on the pathway to transforming our past experiences, they might just be a life saver.

How can your student's past shape their future in a positive rather than negative way?

We Can Help Shape Their Story

In the aftermath of the COVID-19 pandemic, it's crucial we feed young people's internal narrative with hope and belief. *Cradles of Eminence* is a book that outlines the lives of over seven hundred high-achieving individuals. It's interesting to note that of the seven hundred, the vast majority faced tragic hardships early in life. Their narrative, however, was positive: "I will make something of myself in this hardship." How could this be? Once again, there is a common thread. The majority of the high-achieving people had parents who valued education and set an example for a positive narrative.[78] We can do the same today. Instead of the list of victim statements from the beginning of this chapter, what if the Pandemic Population emerged from this pandemic saying:

- "Life is hard, but it's definitely worth it."
- "I will rise up, far above average."
- "I'll find a way to turn this disadvantage into an advantage."
- "I will confidently pursue my goals."

Liam is a university sophomore who returned home when the shelter-in-place order was given on campus. While quarantined at home, he knew he'd have a lot of time on his hands and no parties to attend. His parents saw him pondering how to process this strange season and suggested he could help Carolyn, an eighty-five year old shut-in who had no good way to get food on a regular basis. Liam decided to take groceries to Carolyn and offer her a virtual hug and some friendly conversation. Upon his departure, he wondered how many other elderly people in the area needed the same kind of help. When he discovered the need was tangible, he began an outreach called Invisible Hands. They recruited 3,500 volunteers to deliver food to those who needed it.[79] What an incredible story. All because he chose his narrative. What a way to use a pandemic.

Let me remind you. The question is not if they will carry a narrative inside of them. That part is inevitable. The question is, Will that narrative be one of a victim or one of an overcomer? Will they develop an external locus of control (i.e. "the outcomes of my life are up to external forces") or an internal locus of control (i.e. "the outcomes of my life are up to me")? Will they seize the day or merely size up the day and decide they can't win?

Let me remind you, if we are not intentional with our leadership, there are potential negative long-term outcomes:

- the normalization of isolation
- the normalization of anxiety and fear
- the normalization of a scarcity mindset

If we are intentional in our leadership, however, we can enjoy these positive long-term outcomes:

- the expansion of resourcefulness and innovation
- the expansion of saving and giving
- the expansion of first responders and medical staff

Are you up for this challenge?

It's been said that children have never been good at listening to their elders but they have never failed to emulate them. Our leadership can make or break how Generation Z emerges from this pandemic. What kind of attitudes are we modeling? What example are we setting? What is our narrative that they observe in us on a daily basis?

- Are our motives based in worry or wisdom when we guide them?
- Do we base our foundation upon fear or facts?
- Do we lead them from a place of panic or principles?
- Are we speaking to them out of belief or skepticism?
- Do we model hope or doubt?

The huge question we all must answer is this: What's the story we will all be telling twenty years from now when we look back on this period of time? I hope it will be a story of overcoming and coming together.

Let me illustrate how our narratives are often more impactful than realities. Between 1985 and 1990, crime rates across our country soared. In fact, through the last twenty years of that century, authorities predicted we would see a continued rise in crime, specifically violent crime in major cities. But then—it wasn't so. Crime rates began to drop. And they continued to drop.

According to a 2016 article in *The Atlantic*, "By decade's end, the homicide rate plunged 42 percent nationwide. Violent crime decreased by one-third. What turned into a precipitous decline started later in some areas and took longer in others. But it happened everywhere: in each region of the country, in cities large and small, in rural and urban areas alike."[80]

Believe it or not, we now experience less violent crime in most cities than we did fifty years ago. While there were more mass murders in 2019 than in the past, violent crime overall has been declining for two decades.

So why don't we feel it's in decline?

Our personal narrative says it isn't. We listen to a 24-7 news cycle that repeats the same stories of a single crime over and over again. News feeds often start with this kind of clickbait. Social media posts continue nonstop, repeating a big story until it feels like crime is increasing. Suddenly, it really is—in our minds. News networks are owned by companies with stakeholders who are measuring profits, so increasing viewership is the focus. They need to sell the news, and what news sells better than fear? The greater the disaster, crime, or tragedy, the better.

The bottom line? Our fear narrative continues, and we raise our kids in anxiety and caution because we feel it's true, even when it isn't. Our narrative about what's real is more influential than what's actually real. If we could change our self-talk—the story we are telling ourselves— our kids just might be the greatest beneficiaries.

WHAT THEY NEED TO HEAR

My friend, Collin Sewell, told me his fifteen-year old son recently gave him the greatest compliment. They were in the kitchen talking, and when other family members left the room, Collin's son asked, "Dad, everybody seems stressed out about things right now, don't they?" He was obviously referring to the pandemic and its effect on the economy and public health. Collin responded truthfully, "Well, yes, people are a little worried right now, son."

After a moment's pause, the teen said, "But you're not scared, are you, Dad?"

Collin smiled and said, "No, son, I am not scared."

His son quietly responded, "Good. That's what I thought."

Collin is an intentional dad who's setting a good example. When his son said, "Good. That's what I thought," I believe he was really saying, "Good. That's what I needed to hear."

Let's all be like my friend Collin. Let's lead this pandemic generation well.

TALK IT OVER

1. Which of these strategies seem most relevant and helpful for your situation?

2. What do you think is the narrative your students hold in their head at this time?

3. How could you equip them to tell the right story about this season of their lives?

SEVEN

The Secret Weapon for Leading in Times of Tragedy

Psychologists have long observed that kids tend to do better when their teachers and leaders put the Pygmalion effect to work. This is all about kids' performance matching adult expectations. Students do better when their teacher expects much of them. For years, I assumed there wasn't much difference between having high expectations of students and genuinely believing in students. Both can positively affect them. I now believe, however, that there is a significant difference between the two. Affluent parents may expect a lot of their child because of their own baggage: they don't want to look bad in front of their friends at the country club. This is certainly a case of high expectations, with little regard to belief. Children of certain Asian ethnicities have been known to grow up under "tiger moms" who expect much from them. Some researchers have even drawn connections between the pressure of Asian parents and higher suicide rates in children.[81] Somehow, high expectations backfired. Belief didn't match expectation.

The difference between the two is subtle and can be sinister. An adult leader may assume their high expectations will do the trick in raising a student performance. What we must realize is that expectations are only half of the equation.

Let's examine the other side.

GREAT EXPECTATIONS

The impact of faculty expectations came to light in 1968, when Robert Rosenthal and Lenore Jacobson's study, published in their book

Pygmalion in the Classroom: Teacher Expectation and Pupils Intellectual Development, revealed that if teachers expected an enhanced level of performance from their pupils, the pupil's performance improved. This study supported the hypothesis that reality can be positively or negatively influenced by the expectations of others and was called the observer-expectancy effect. Rosenthal argued that biased expectancies could affect results and create self-fulfilling prophecies.[82] The research actually began with lab rats and college students. One group of students were told they'd been given a DNA strain of genius rats; those rats should make it through the maze efficiently. Another group was told their rats had average intelligence, so the results would likely be mixed. As you might guess, the "genius rats" outperformed the average ones measurably and consistently. In the end, the experiment was actually on the rats, not the rats. The reality was, there were no genius rats. It was a random sampling of rodents in both groups. The difference, however, showed up in how those rats were led and treated. Time and time again, the power of expectations influenced the outcomes. The students who were told they were working with genius rats treated them more warmly, spoke to them more kindly, and encouraged them more often to reach the goal.[83]

Later, when the experiments were transferred to teachers and students, the same results occurred. When teachers believed they had high-performing students, those faculty members continued to encourage them and push them toward their perceived potential, even if the kids were a bit rebellious in the classroom. Their teachers were more patient and better listeners. As you may have guessed, the experiment was actually done on a random sampling of students. Both groups contained average-performing students, but the classroom led by a teacher with high expectations outperformed the other group every time. In the end, the teacher's expectations influenced the scores of the students.[84]

This phenomenon became known as the Pygmalion effect. It's named after the Greek mythological figure Pygmalion, a sculptor who fell in love with a statue he had carved name Galatea. He loved it so much that it became real to him. Her beauty drove him to pray to the goddess Aphrodite to give life to the figurine. When his hopes and expectations rose high enough, Galatea became real and the two married. His expectations brought life to the statue. It was driven, however, by his own expectations and imagination.

Herein lies the weakness of mere expectation.

While people do tend to live up to or down to another's expectations, it can have an unhealthy effect. In my survey of Generation Z high school students, they listed their second greatest source of stress was parental expectations. Most of them openly shared their high respect for mom and dad but were acutely aware of their parents' assumptions that they should score well on tests, achieve a high GPA, and get accepted into a great college. Their expectations, while well intended, created a pressure on the kids that fostered deeper stress and anxiety. In short, sometimes our anticipation for Generation Z can cultivate anxiety in them.

So, how does a teacher, coach, or parent ensure their expectations generate positive outcomes?

The truth is that we can't guarantee anything. Sometimes, well-intended wishes, hopes, dreams, and expectations produce negative emotional responses. It depends on the personality of the child and the context of our expectations. There is, however, a way to put the odds in their favor.

THE SECRET OF EXPRESSING BELIEF

A group of psychologists from Stanford, Yale, Columbia, and other higher-education institutions set out to explore how teachers could offer feedback that would elicit the best effort from students in their middle school classrooms. Researchers had teachers give a writing assignment to their students, after which students were given various types of feedback. To their surprise, researchers found there was one type of feedback that improved student effort to such a degree that they called it "magical." Students who received this feedback chose to revise their essay far more often than students who got different feedback. Effort rose a minimum of 40 percent among white students; and a 320 percent boost among black students. The study here[85] seems to answer the expectations dilemma. The feedback was simply:

"I am giving these comments because I have high expectations of you, and I know you can reach them."

Notice how expectations are combined with belief. Added to "high expectations" is the phrase "I know you can reach them." It's a statement of belonging and belief as well as expectation. You're good enough to be here. And the results were clear. Students responded.[86]

Let's look at why this is so vital right now.

When belief and expectation match, it creates the potential for the greatest impact on student performance. The US Department of Education undertook a huge project called the Early Childhood Longitudinal Study (ECLS) over twenty years ago. The ECLS attempted to measure the academic progress of children from kindergarten to the fifth grade. While it's difficult to fully distinguish between correlation and causality, it is vividly apparent that one gigantic factor is the education levels of a child's parents. If a child is raised in a home where parents just don't expect a child to do well or to go on to college, the child is less like to do so. If a child is raised where that is the common expectation and belief, the child is more likely to do so.[87]

In a 2014 study, the same results occurred, and the causality was even more clear. High school students were given comments after turning in an essay in a literature class. Feedback was given to each student, but half of the students had one sentence added at the bottom:

"I am giving you this feedback because I believe in you."

There is the phrase plain and simple: "I believe in you." According to researchers Cohen and Garcia, students who received this sentence not only performed better immediately afterward, but also scored at higher levels a year later.[88] Once again, the effect was more significant for students of color who often feel less valued by their teachers. Frequently, teachers can communicate positive expectations and belief to students by using encouraging words. It is easy to do this with students who appear motivated, who learn easily, or who are quick. It is even more important, however, to communicate positive beliefs and expectations to students who are slow, appear unmotivated, or are struggling.

WHEN OUR LEADERSHIP IS UNHEALTHY

Expectations can be silent, but they are still real. And kids can sense them. Our expectations nudge children in certain directions because, quite frankly, kids often intuitively trust an adult's perception of reality more than their own. Yet, as we've noted, expectations can have a downside. If expectations are the only factor in a child's performance, eventually they can negatively influence that child's mental health. We see this play out on a daily basis:

- Parents who are living out their unlived life through their children can push the children to perform because of their own emotional deficits. It's about their baggage.
- Parents who don't want to appear to be bad parents among their social network can add undue stress. Their ego is in play. It's about the family's image.
- Parents who want their children to do what they did, gaining a 4.0 GPA in the classroom or securing a starting spot on the basketball team, can project their achievements onto their children.

Our unhealthy motivations infect a child's mindset. In fact, they're contagious. While kids may not understand why we lead the way we do at first, eventually their social intelligence will kick in and they'll begin to resent the parent or teacher who leads from an egocentric motivation. They can start overfunctioning or underperforming due to wrong motives. The best remedy I have found is to check my motives. While this method is not foolproof, it's a great place to start. When my two children were in K–12 education, I performed daily motive checks on my own behavior. Answering these questions was crucial for me:

1. Why did I do certain things for them?
2. Why did I say certain things to them?
3. Why did I expect specific results from them?
4. Why did I want them to achieve particular goals?

As a kid, I loved sports. I still do. I played basketball and baseball and ran track. For many years, my life revolved around playing sports and staying up on all the statistics of our school's teams and our city's professional teams. Naturally, when my son was born, I imagined us playing catch in the backyard or me watching him play basketball and cheering him on from the stands.

It was only in my imagination.

I remember teaching Jonathan to hit a baseball and standing so close to him before I pitched the ball, I could almost touch him. It just didn't come natural. He later told me he wanted to try out for little league baseball. I coached the team with a neighbor friend of mine, and I'll never forget watching Jonathan standing out in left field, staring at his baseball mitt or watching butterflies as they fluttered by. He couldn't have been more disinterested. He later played soccer and other sports, but it was never his first love. He tried, but nothing caught on.

I later found out—*he was doing it for me.*

He knew how much his father loved sports and assumed I expected him to love them too. He wanted to please me so much, he forced himself to try to play for me. When I recognized this, I assured him I only wanted him to take on the extracurricular activities he enjoyed doing. I would get involved in what he wanted to do, not vice versa. It wasn't long before our entire family recognized he was a thespian. He loved theatre and all that came with it—rehearsals, blocking, memorizing his lines, acting, projecting from the stage, making people laugh, singing, you name it. And he was amazing. It was intuitive for him. Several times he played the lead role in a community theatre program. For me, the sequence went like this:

- When it came to sports, I had expectations but no belief.
- Later, I dropped my expectations and focused on my belief in him.
- Eventually, I had both high expectations and belief in him when it came to theatre.

GETTING IT RIGHT

Both expectations and belief can positively affect outcomes, but one without the other is incomplete and can lead to an unhealthy mental state in the students we lead. Ideally, high expectations play a positive role in a child's performance when we follow a few rules:

1. The expectations are matched with their potential.
2. The expectations are birthed from healthy motivations.

3. The expectations are combined with belief in them.
4. The expectations and belief are delivered through a relationship.

Naturally, there are times when, through our high expectations, we must raise their expectations of themselves. This is important, even when it's not a subject they are passionate about such as math or literature. In those times, we must adjust our expectations to a level where we inspire them to give their best effort but don't expect them to become Albert Einstein or Robert Frost. In short, our expectations must correspond to their capacity in any given area.

May I suggest a metaphor that has helped me? To lead them well, I believe we must become velvet-covered bricks.

The velvet-covered brick is one of our leadership images. We call them *Habitudes: Images that Form Leadership Habits and Attitudes®*. This metaphor captures what effective leaders do when leading students, especially those in Generation Z. Picture a brick covered in velvet. Both elements represent an ingredient in great leaders. One is about expectations. The other is about belief.

Velvet communicates "I accept you as you are. I'm attentive to you. I understand you. I empathize with you. I care for you, and I support you." In short, "I believe in you."

Brick communicates "Because I believe in you, I hold a high standard for you to reach. I won't lower it because it feels difficult." In short, "I expect much from you."

Consider for a moment what it feels like when a parent or teacher lowers the expectation of a student or, even worse, does the work for their student. At first it feels great. Who doesn't love a day made easier? Over time, however, it begins to backfire. The students think the adult really doesn't think they have it in them to pull off the goal by themselves. They begin lowering their own expectations of themselves. They start thinking less of themselves. They believe they need someone to help them perform well. This is not a good habit to take to college. When we lower expectations, it automatically signals low belief. They need a velvet-covered brick to lead them:

Velvet = Belief
Brick = Expectation

This embodies leadership that is both *responsive* and *demanding*. According to well-known research from Diana Baumrind at U C Berkeley, kids need both from adults, not one or the other.[89] When we are responsive to them and their needs, we earn the right to be demanding of them and their potential. Ideally, velvet should precede brick. When we lead this way, it naturally cultivates a "growth mindset" in students.

As I noted earlier in this book, Stanford psychologist Carol Dweck coined the terms, "fixed mindset" and "growth mindset." A fixed mind believes "I am either good at math, or I'm not." It's fixed. A growth mindset believes the brain is like a muscle and can get stronger. This person may commonly use the term yet. This person might say, "I am not good at math yet."[90] I have seen belief and expectation cultivate a growth mindset in thousands of students over the last forty years.

THE STEPS TO ESTABLISH BOTH BELIEF AND EXPECTATIONS

Expectation without belief is incomplete. As I've mentioned, if I have high expectations but I don't believe in the student in front of me, it just feels harsh. But if I say I believe in that student in front of me, yet I don't expect much of her, it makes my belief feel artificial and hollow. The combination of the two is our secret weapon. So, how do we walk this line? Let me suggest a few steps we can take.

Action Steps

1. **Spend one-on-one time with the student to build a relationship.**

   Students learn best from a teacher that they believe likes them. In your time together, ask questions that deepen trust and awareness. Spending time with a student silently communicates belief. You're saying, *"I like who you are."*

2. **Identify their strengths.**

   When a leader discovers the strengths of a student, belief in the student naturally follows. Not only that, but the belief is also not disingenuous; it is built off of real data. The leader can authentically affirm belief because he or she has witnessed the student's potential. This answers the question lurking inside the student: *Has anyone noticed what I can do?*

3. Tie your words of affirmation and belief into a student's natural strengths, so your words come across as accurate.

This may be essential because the student may also see this strength but may value your assessment more than his or her own. This answers the question every young person silently asks themselves: *Do I have what it takes?*

4. Be specific.

At first, words of belief should be offered as specifically as possible. Note particular elements in them you find above average or even outstanding. Once you've pointed out specific traits or skills, you can move toward general words of belief. This answers another question students ask themselves: *Am I unique?*

5. Finally, help them imagine a preferred future.

Cast a vision for what they could do with their strengths, talents, and unique qualities. Talk about outcomes, then the inputs needed to achieve those outcomes. Paint the picture that if they'll work hard at A, B, and C, it could get them X, Y, and Z. This is the ultimate result of both expectation and belief. It answers the question: *Can I go far?*

I mentioned my son Jonathan earlier. It would have been fruitless to tell him he was awesome at baseball when he wasn't. That hyperbole is hollow and even damaging to kids. However, once we tied in belief and expectations to who he was—it bore lots of fruit. Jonathan's love for acting and drama has actually fueled his college degree and career choice. He majored in screenwriting and has since become a writer of scripts. He has exceeded his parents' expectations—but not our belief.

Once we saw it in him, we knew he could do it. It was easy to believe in him.

TALK IT OVER

1. What are your thoughts and experience about expectations and belief?

2. How have you seen the impact of high or low expectations of students?

3. Which are you stronger in communicating to students—expectations or belief?

4. What action steps should you take to match expectations and beliefs in your students?

EIGHT

Eight Strategies to Lead Generation Z Through the Coronavirus

There is an urban legend about two men who were hospitalized with terminal diseases. They shared a room, but the bed of one of the patients sat right next to the window. Each day, that man would describe to his roommate what he saw as he looked out the window: lovers walking hand in hand, children eating ice cream cones or flying kites, pet owners walking their dogs in the park and playing fetch with them. As each day passed, the other patient grew more jealous that he was unable to see these lovely items, since his bed sat next to a wall. He soon became bitter.

Sometime later, the man positioned next to the window died in his sleep. As soon as his body was removed from the hospital room, his fellow patient requested he be moved to the other bed. When he was, he was startled. As he looked out the window, he realized it faced a blank wall.

Everything the other gentleman saw, came from his own imagination.

Throughout this book, I've been reinforcing the impact of our personal narrative. Not only did the Great Depression kids get through hardship because of their positive, can-do attitudes, they passed those same narratives to others, making all the difference in the world. Their story proves to us an important truth: *The personal story we tell ourselves about what happens is even more important than what actually happens.* I am not suggesting we lie to ourselves and fake being happy. I'm suggesting we see the positive angle in every experience and tell ourselves that better story. My mother modeled this so well for me that I picked it up naturally. She emerged from the Great Depression grateful and satisfied with the smallest of blessings. When I went off to college, I took that same spirit with me, to the point that my classmate, Russ, told me one day, "Tim, you'd be fine even if you were poor. You always think you're fortunate."

Coming by this perspective wasn't hard for me. I knew who I wanted to become.

You see, if a young person is clear on who they want to become and what they want their future to hold, it will inform how they interpret life's hardships. Their perspective will be leveraged to help them grow from anything. "There are many ways to think and talk about one's experiences in life," writes Dr. Nick Hobson in *Psychology Today*. "These personal narratives allow us to reflect on both our triumphs and shortcomings, and tailor our current beliefs and actions to fit our future goals."[91]

We will become the sum total of the personal narratives we have for ourselves.

BUILDING A BETTER NARRATIVE IDENTITY

Narrative identity is a relatively new term. Developed by psychologists Dan McAdams and Kate McLean, "narrative identity is a person's internalized and evolving life story, integrating the reconstructed past and imagined future to provide life with some degree of unity and purpose."[92]

The best news of all is that we can play a big part in a student's narrative.

Researchers from the world of behavioral science have concluded that "narrators who find redemptive meanings in suffering and adversity, and who construct life stories that feature themes of personal agency and exploration, tend to enjoy higher levels of mental health, well-being, and maturity. Researchers have tracked the development of narrative identity from its origins in conversations between parents and their young children to the articulation of sophisticated meaning-making strategies in the personal stories told in adolescence and the emerging adulthood years."[93]

In short, we play a larger role than we may realize in framing the stories of the students we lead.

This is what this chapter is all about—helping the Pandemic Population frame their story. As I watch and listen to parents, teachers, coaches, and employers during the coronavirus outbreak, I have specifically listened to how their leadership has been affecting kids. Sadly, it has not been helpful in shaping a good "comeback" story in them.

I think I know why.

Let me tell you what's more contagious than the coronavirus in our country: fear. It's infectious, and I believe it's doing more damage overall to the kids in Generation Z than a virus. Sadly, they are "catching" our anxiety. We panic far too easy. We fall into a scarcity mindset. We make mountains out of molehills. And it's not helping the mental health of our youth.

Police in Newport, Oregon, posted a Facebook message to citizens in their area: "It's hard to believe we even have to post this. Do NOT call 9-1-1 just because you ran out of toilet paper. You will survive without our assistance."[94]

Two moms squabbled over paper-towel packages at our local grocery store in Atlanta. Their children watched their immature behavior until a clerk broke up the fight. It's no wonder schools struggle with bullying and poor civility among students.

Some parents aren't allowing their kids to even go outside for fear of the coronavirus. Those kids, understandably, are going stir crazy inside the house all day. When we find ourselves in unfamiliar territory, too often we panic.

As McAdams describes narrative identity—the internalized story you create about yourself—he calls it your own "personal myth." Today, our personal myths are far more anxious, even paranoid. Past generations have been through worse times with less, but they still carried a can-do attitude. Today, we are much more emotionally fragile. Greg Lukianoff and Jonathan Haidt, in their book, *The Coddling of the American Mind*, point out that much smaller hardships can send us into a tailspin.[95]

So, before we dig into how we help Generation Z shape their story, let's begin with us. Below I offer three questions to ask yourself as you endure today's coronavirus pandemic.

Three Questions to Ask Yourself About Your Message to Kids:

1. **Check your motive:** *Am I communicating worry or wisdom to them?*

   Motives can be seen by young people. They know when a teacher is frustrated or when a mom is paranoid. Sometimes it comes out in our words. We say things like, "Don't go outside! I don't want you catching that virus and going to the emergency room." Or kids watch us hoard toilet paper like it's going out of style to the point that grocery stores began to limit the volume customers can buy. This stockpiling is not only unnecessary, it also relays to kids our worry-based leadership. While "there is no evidence that children are more prone to contracting COVID-19," according to the CDC, there is plenty of evidence that today's kids are vulnerable to angst.[96]

2. **Check your foundation:** *Do I base my conclusions on fear or facts?*

   Are your conclusions based upon a hyped media broadcast or a social media post created to be click bait for viewers? Do you buy into anxious speculation rather than accurate information? As COVID-19 spread, the US surgeon general warned that people were buying masks so rapidly that healthcare providers were finding them hard to obtain and it put communities at risk. While we are all making anxious decisions based on less than reliable information, The Washington Post reminds us of the simple truth: "The virus may be novel, but you really don't need to buy anything new or special to brace for it. *The Washington Post* spoke to epidemiology experts, and they said the most important aspect of preparedness costs nothing at all — calm."[97]

3. **Check your advice:** *Do I base my leadership on panic or principles?*

   When we don't possess a set of principles by which we lead, teach, or parent our kids, we tend to be reactionary. In today's environment, a lack of principle means we often panic based on the anxiety happening around us. We catch it, then our kids catch it from us. "Don't panic," said Timothy Brewer, professor of epidemiology and medicine at UCLA. "There's no value in panicking or telling people to be afraid. Don't let fear and emotion drive the response to this virus. That can be extremely difficult because it is new, and we're still learning about it, but don't allow fear of what we don't know about the virus to overwhelm what we do know."[98]

Are you guilty of worry, fear, or panic when you lead kids? How could you change that?

Four Steps to Equipping Students to Form Their Identity

Now, let's look at the process of shaping the narrative of the next generation under our care. Life coach and author Greg Nelson suggests the following steps to develop the right personal narratives:

1. **Identify the student's current story.**

   Ask them, How would you describe the narrative you are telling yourself? What words do you use? Are they emotionally charged words? Are they descriptive?

2. **Evaluate the content of their current story.**

   Is what they're telling themselves empowering or disempowering them? Does it limit their belief in themselves? Is it influenced by a wider story about others?

3. **Characterize the effects (outcomes) of their current story.**

   What does the story do to them? Does it cause their attitude to spiral downward or upward? Is it helping them make progress? Is it hindering progress? Does it excite them?

4. **Reframe their story with new metaphors.**[99]

   This isn't just trying to make them feel better. It must be authentic to transform them. It means looking at themselves from a new angle and creating a picture to frame it.

Let me offer you an illustration to spur you on.

Nathan was a senior in high school in the spring of 2020 when he, like millions of other students, felt penalized by the COVID-19 pandemic. It wasn't that he couldn't experience a normal day, but his internal story was like many other students: "I've fallen behind. I don't know if I can catch up. Life is hard, and I don't know if it's worth starting all over with my dreams."

It is easy to see the kernel of truth in this statement and why he'd embrace it.

To try and help, I spoke to Nathan and walked through the four steps outlined above. We first began to identify the story he was telling himself. I empathized with him, saying I could understand why he felt that way. Once we put our finger on his story, however, we engaged in a fascinating conversation about how it was affecting him. After some reflection he admitted it was having a negative effect on his attitude and ambition. We then moved on to step three. He was quickly able to identify the natural outcomes:

- His drive to hunt for a job was diminished.
- He felt unhappy most of the time.
- He wasn't working out the way he used to do.
- He failed to make plans or even pursue his former plans.

He clearly needed a new story, framed by a new metaphor.

The new metaphor we agreed upon is one of our new *Habitudes*®. The metaphor is simply "Candles and Brushfires." Stop and think about these two types of flames. Both represent fire, but they respond very differently to harsh winds. A candle can be extinguished by a small breath at a birthday party. It doesn't take much to blow them out. A brushfire, on the other hand, not only survives harsh winds but also gets stronger. The same wind that extinguishes a candle extends a brushfire.

An ancient Chinese proverb says, "When the winds of change blow, some people build walls and others build windmills." This simply means some people shift into survival mode (putting up a wall to hold on) and others actually put that harsh wind to work on their behalf.

Nathan's new metaphor was to be a brushfire not a candle and his motto was "Chase the wind." By this, he means he plans to actually see which way the wind is blowing and capture that momentum for himself. I love it.

Keep in mind, adversity can be a friend when we ensure one condition.

Making Stress Help Them, Not Harm Them

Psychologist Donna Jackson Nakazawa reminds us, "In 1995, physicians Vincent Felitti and Robert Anda launched a large-scale epidemiological study that probed the child and adolescent histories of 17,000 subjects, comparing their childhood experiences to their later adult health records. The results were shocking: Nearly two-thirds of individuals had encountered one or more Adverse Childhood Experiences (ACEs)—a term Felitti and Anda coined to encompass the chronic, unpredictable, and stress-inducing events some children face."[100] Chronic stressors include divorce, neglect, abuse, and parents with addictions or mental illness.

This research, plus a study done at Yale University more recently, reveal two conclusions that should inform how we lead and mentor students today.[101]

First, for the most part, youth exposed to adversity while growing up actually become stronger for having experienced it. Their emotional muscles grow resilient. Without these stressors, or when adults rescue kids from such stressors, they begin to give up more quickly, believing they need adults around to save them from hardship. Youth are naturally antifragile, and it is adults who make them fragile over time.

Second, it is only when the stressors become toxic and chronic (continuing for years) that children begin to surrender their will and stop trying. "When we're thrust over and over again into stress-inducing situations during childhood or adolescence, our physiological stress response shifts into overdrive, and we lose the ability to respond appropriately and effectively to future stressors—10, 20, even 30 years later."[102]

The Difference Between the Two Outcomes?

- Kids who give up have endured *chronic stressors* with no adult who offers them hope. They feel they are alone and there's no hope or help.

- Kids who grow stronger experience *periodical stressors*, yet have adults who encourage them to continue. They learn they can change their reality.

How would you describe the stressors of your Generation Z young person? How can you help?

EIGHT STRATEGIES TO LEAD GENERATION Z THROUGH THE CORONAVIRUS

Before we close this chapter, and for that matter this book, I want to summarize the strategies we've discussed. While this list won't encapsulate everything I've shared with you, this information will be my most condensed recommendation for you and your leadership. So, let's examine these eight practices you can build into the habits and attitudes of your students that will enable them to form a positive growth narrative:

1. **Make a habit of talking about the silver lining.**
   This proved to be helpful for me when my parents raised me and for my two kids as they grew up. We've all heard the phrase, "Every cloud has a silver lining." Begin to condition your students to look for it. When my daughter Bethany was seven, she was eating breakfast with her brother, Jonathan. He was eating his favorite—cinnamon toast—but I had made it using bread that had seeds on the crust. He didn't care for the seeds. I remember Bethany saying to him, "Jonathan, keep your eye on the cinnamon not on the seeds." We all helped each other spot the upside to every downturn.

2. **Break down the hardship into digestible bites in their minds.**
   Hardship becomes harder when its overwhelming. Just like we used to cut our kids' food into bites, we must do this mentally with tough times. As with food, the younger the child, the smaller the bites must be. Sit down and discuss what's overwhelming them. Then, help them break it down into daily challenges. Clarify for them the doable tasks. When a kid is scared, the amygdala in his or her brain kicks in and sends messages: fight, flight, or freeze. In

these times, the science project or the college application or the job interview must be broken down for logic to return.

3. Identify any cognitive distortions or conformation bias in their narratives.

Our brains play tricks on us when we're anxious or afraid. Confirmation bias occurs when we naturally migrate toward information that confirms what we already think. These assumptions can prevent us from seeing the truth. Cognitive distortions are assumptions based on emotional biases, like the "bandwagon bias" which is the belief that something is right because so many of their peers are doing it; or the "anchoring bias" which is dependent on the first fact mentioned instead of looking deeper at the facts. Check to see if you or your young person have fallen prey to them. (See the Appendix for additional insights on conformation bias.)

4. Remind them of past personal successes.

Most of us have selective memories. We forget certain facts or details based on our bias or what moved us emotionally at the time. It is important to remind your students of past successes they've experienced that could inform their future story. I recall sitting down with each of my kids in years gone by and reminding them what they'd done in the past that was reason enough to suggest they could "win" again—trophies, good grades, championships, recitals, school plays, and science projects.

5. Help them practice psychological distancing.

This is a term from Yale professor Marc Brackett. Ask students to think of a friend who's struggling with anxiety over COVID-19 or with a challenge in front of him or her. Then inquire what advice they would they give their friend? Finally—ask if they practice their own advice. Often, kids know what's right but fail to apply it. It is almost always helpful to step back from our own fears and pretend they belong to someone else. We become more objective. The key is to follow the very advice we'd give a friend.

6. **Tell stories of those who turned disadvantages into advantages.**

   Earlier in this book, I mentioned how Isaac Newton made the most of the Great Plague of London in 1665. I also mentioned a boxer, Gene Tunney, who won a championship because of a bad break. There are loads of stories from history of people who took advantage of a disadvantage—and those stories need to be retold to Generation Z. I loved Malcolm Gladwell's book *David and Goliath*. He poses the question, While David certainly had great faith, wasn't he ultimately able to defeat the giant because he saw his own advantage? Goliath was infantry. David was artillery. He was able to toss a stone from his sling from far way and win.

7. **Express both high belief and high expectations.**

   This strategy will not surprise you, since we discussed this in the last chapter. A study found that students perform better on standardized tests each year when their teachers are tough graders. This study also argues that when students have the mindset that says "everybody gets a gold star," it does "more damage than good." This report, published by the Thomas B. Fordham Institute, found this effect holds true for students across ethnic groups, gender, and socioeconomic makeup or prior academic background.[103] What's more, the study also found evidence of long-term learning gains for students. Always hold both high expectations and belief for your students.

8. **Practice affirming self-talk.**

   Finally, while most people talk to themselves (at least a little bit) each day, too many of us express how frustrated we are at ourselves or what an "idiot" we were for making that last statement. Build a habit of positive and affirming self-talk. Confirm that you know you can do this, that you can learn and grow into the challenge in front of you. Edmond Mbiaka says, "Consistent positive self-talk is unquestionably one of the greatest gifts to one's subconscious mind."[104] The most successful NCAA athletes tend to tell themselves before a big game: "I got this!" Zig Ziglar once joked about how he loved talking to himself, saying there were two big reasons he did: "I love talking to intelligent people," he would say. "I also love hearing intelligent people talk."

WHAT WILL WE REMEMBER FROM THIS PANDEMIC?

Allow me to summarize my greatest concern and my greatest goal for the pandemic population. A few years ago, my extended family gathered for a reunion. My sisters and I reminisced about our childhoods, including vacations, past girlfriends and boyfriends, squabbles we had, you name it. What struck me that day was, while we all remembered the most significant occasions, we each recalled different details and more specific stories.

The fact is, behavioral scientists have gathered a body of research that suggests our memories are not only fallible, they can be downright inaccurate and even reconstructed. For example, my sister and I recall a very different upbringing, even though we grew up in same home. Our recollections of our dad are similar, but we drew different conclusions. She and I have both unwittingly reordered our mental libraries of what happened.

Reconstructing Our Memories

More than we realize, our memories play tricks on us. Sometimes, we do it to ourselves. Researchers have come to realize that memories are created over time from our perceptions of reality. An episode of a National Public Radio podcast, HIDDEN BRAIN, talks about this idea. It's called "Did That Really Happen?" Even the conversations we have or the media we consume after an event has occurred can reshape our recollection of it. Of course, that's not the way it feels inside our heads. Many of us trust our memories, especially of significant events. So, let's break down how this happens. Memories are affected by:

- *Expectations*—Our memories are colored by what we expected to happen.
- *Imaginations*—Our version of reality is shaped in our minds with each story we tell.
- *Preconceived notions*—We look for confirmation bias, and life seems to reaffirm it.

- *Emotions*—The level of emotion we feel in the moment influences our memory of it.[105]

In addition to that, our mood, our sleep levels, our personality all play a role in exactly what we remember. This will be key to leading students to base their memories on fact and to construct a healthy memory of this pandemic. It could make or break their future.

The key will be enabling them to retain an accurate memory but a positive narrative.

My goal is to help you lead students well. Our job as parents, teachers, coaches and employers is to equip them to think and act in a way that's hopeful. Where there is no hope in the future, there is no power in the present.

About halfway through the COVID-19 pandemic and the protests on behalf of George Floyd, I began seeing people post on social media that maybe we should just cancel 2020. It was already such a difficult year. I have a different take on it all. It was voiced in a quote I came across on social media. It went something like this:

What if 2020 isn't cancelled?

What if 2020 is the year we've all been waiting for?

A year so uncomfortable, so painful, so scary, so raw—

That it finally forces us to grow.

A year that screams so loud it finally awakens us from our ignorant slumber.

A year we finally accept the need for change.

Declare change. Work for change. Become the change.

A year we finally band together, instead of pushing each other apart.[106]

TALK IT OVER

1. How would you summarize the "current story" your students are telling themselves?

2. How have you added to that narrative?

3. What steps from this chapter do you want to start taking? How will they add value?

Tools and Resources to Equip the Pandemic Population

What Do Young People Need from Their Leader Most?

Leaders must remember first and foremost that people (including kids) under their care have very different temperaments and will react to these times differently. Be careful that you don't minimize the angst others are feeling, while at the same time you act as a source of steady hope. People need three items most from their leader during this season. They spell the word: CAB. I tell myself to jump in a CAB every day I am interacting with others:

Context

It's easy for young people to watch the news all day and get freaked out. They feel angst from all the bad news and the uncertainty of the season. Good leaders explain both the problems and the context for those problems. No matter the crisis, it is likely not the worst crisis we have ever faced, yet the problem in front of us does deserve our focused attention. Context means you furnish perspective on what's happening, you stay knowledgeable on current details, and you become a source of wisdom, especially for those who fall on either end of the spectrum—those who feel it's no big deal and those who feel like the sky is falling.

Applications

People usually need leaders to offer practical action steps during this time. It may sound silly, but sometimes grown adults need reminders of the applications we've been given to respond to COVID-19 well: wash your hands many times a day, stay six feet apart from others in public, wear a mask outside, and shelter in place when you can. The best leaders leave people with clear applications for their day. In fact, clarity on what to do is the greatest gift a leader can offer right now.

Belief

Napoleon Bonaparte said, "Leaders are dealers in hope." I believe we owe it to our people in uncertain times to offer belief and hope for a better future. This season will one day pass and we may just return to a better normal. I actually believe this. Americans, still in some ways polarized, are now cooperating and focusing on helping each other. Together, for instance, we applauded health care professionals and first responders. Belief brings people together. Share a positive message: we will get through this and be better for it.

Tools and Resources

I would be remiss if I didn't offer some tools for you to use as you lead this young population to recover and to flourish in this post-pandemic period. Here are a few resources Growing Leaders has put together that can help as you work to lead the Pandemic Population.

Home Chats

These are eight discussion guides you can download for free. Each guide is anchored by a *Habitude®* image. In these guides, you'll spark conversation based on an image, discussion questions, an activity, and a summary of the big idea.
Visit: *GrowingLeaders.com/HomeChats*

Habitudes® for Social and Emotional Learning

You've likely heard of social and emotional learning. These are the soft skills students need to embrace a positive self-narrative and to establish positive habits that will help them thrive as an emerging adult. It's all based around helping them build emotional intelligence and social intelligence. These enable them to apply self-awareness, self-management, social awareness, relationship building, and responsible decision-making. We've created an engaging curriculum called *Habitudes for*

Social and Emotional Learning. This multi-year program is now being used by hundreds of middle and high schools across the country.
Visit: *GrowingLeaders.com/SEL*

The MPACT App

Growing Leaders is partnering with the MPACT app to offer free content and activities that you and your Generation Z students can access. MPACT is a challenge not only to learn the principles of leadership and social and emotional learning but also to apply them as well.

Download the MPACT App in the Apple or Google App store and select "A Better You" to access this free content.

Helping Students Recognize Cognitive Bias

Most of you who read this article are leaders. You lead schools, businesses, sports teams, and families. Many of you work with student leaders and want to help them navigate the privileges and responsibilities of their position.

I recently sat in on a Student Government Association meeting on a college campus. It was immediately clear these were intelligent and active university students. In the course of the meeting, however, I also recognized that these students suffered from cognitive bias. In one discussion, the students became divided and even irate about an outside speaker who'd been invited onto the campus. Instead of conducting a rational conversation, these smart students displayed their emotional biases, shouting at one another in ways that didn't even make sense.

What is cognitive bias, you ask?

Cognitive bias is a term used by those in the field of psychology to describe the fallible thought processes we unintentionally practice. The human brain is capable of incredible ideation, but it's also capable of flawed thinking, brought on by hidden emotional distortions. The fact is, we all make various kinds of mental mistakes, called cognitive biases, which can affect our decisions and actions. These biases extrapolate information from wrong sources and poor memories, often with the goal of confirming pre-existing beliefs.

Experts in the social sciences have identified 188 known confirmation biases. Each leads us to deviate from making rational and accurate judgments. Below are some of the more common cognitive biases I see when I meet with high school and college students:

- *Familiarity bias:* when we place our trust in the limited experience we have rather than seeking the obvious benefits of gathering information.
- *Self-Attribution bias:* when we attribute our club's success to ourselves instead of exterior factors like our team, luck, trends, or timing. In contrast, when things go wrong for these same people, they look outside for an explanation.
- *Anchoring bias*: when we're too dependent on the first fact or number mentioned, instead of rationally examining a range of options and information.
- *Survivorship bias:* the assumption that entrepreneurship must be easy since there are so many startups, forgetting that the majority failed and are no longer around.
- *Bandwagon bias:* when we believe something is right to do because so many other people are doing it. This is the proverbial cliff all our friends are jumping off of.

HELPING STUDENTS RISE ABOVE COGNITIVE BIAS

Unfortunately, today's adult population often struggles as much with cognitive bias as kids do. We fail to remain objective and logical because our emotions or faulty memories fail us. Most of the time, our bias actually stems from remembering an event or discussion in a distorted way, and then each time we recount it, our narrative continues to evolve.

It happens all the time. So, what do we do?

Seven Ideas to Help Student Leaders with Cognitive Bias

1. **Discuss the presence of cognitive bias in everyone.**
   Often, the best first step is to expose your student leaders (or debate team) to the reality of cognitive bias. Many ideas on this list may seem like to strong of a step to take, but I recommend you never neglect to at least make students aware that bias happens to all of us. Illustrate how memories fail us and emotions often rule us.

2. Utilize training and controlled processing with students.

Training has also shown to reduce cognitive bias. Carey K. Morewedge and colleagues found that research participants exposed to one-shot training interventions, such as educational videos and debiasing games that taught mitigating strategies, exhibited significant reductions in their commission of six cognitive biases for up to three months.[107]

3. Leverage psychological tools with the students.

There are some tools leaders can capitalize on when working with young leaders today. Check out cognitive bias mitigation and cognitive bias modification. Both of these ideas refer to the process of reducing cognitive biases in people and also refer to a growing area of psychological therapies for anxiety, depression, and addiction called CBMT.

4. Utilize an outside moderator as a discussion referee.

A person who sits in as a moderator or a sort of referee—someone who is objective and has no dog in the fight—can serve as an impartial listener and call out when they hear or observe cognitive bias in any party. This individual can serve to umpire emotional arguments and help to maintain rational thoughts and decisions.

5. Record important conversations and decisions.

When meetings end, but attendees remember the conversations differently, it's often because of our cognitive biases when it comes to memory. People just have flawed memories. One solution can be to record the meetings and play them back later.

6. Train students in how to think critically.

One great long-term remedy for cognitive distortions is teaching students critical thinking. Too many higher education faculty tell me their freshman still haven't learned to be critical thinkers—who evaluate an issue from all sides, ask intelligent questions and draw an objective conclusion. Its best to begin doing this with non-emotional issues.

7. Use Reference Class Forecasting

Reference class forecasting is a method for systematically debiasing estimates and decisions, based on what Daniel Kahneman has dubbed the outside view.[108] It is amusing to note that neither our US adult or student population still do not do this well.

End Notes

CHAPTER ONE

1. Hannah Ritchie, et al., "Terrorism," Our World in Data, July 28, 2013, https://ourworldindata.org/terrorism#all-charts-preview.

2. Ritchie, et al., "Terrorism."

3. Renee Ruchotzke, "Working At Cross-Purposes," Unitarian Universalist Association, August 28, 2018. www.uua.org/leadership/library/leadership-technical-skills-working-at-cross-purposes.

4. Celia Tulk and Philanthropy Media Network, "Six Ways to Separate Your Kids from Their Phones," Growing Leaders, July 30, 2019, https://growingleaders.com/blog/six-ways-to-separate-your-kids-from-their-phones.

5. Zack Friedman, "Student Loan Debt Statistics in 2019: A $1.5 Trillion Crisis," Forbes, October 14, 2019, www.forbes.com/sites/zackfriedman/2019/02/25/student-loan-debt-statistics-2019/#7cc45abb133f.

6. Friedman, "Student Loan."

7. Chris Nichols, "PolitiFact - How Is a 'Mass Shooting' Defined?," PolitiFact, October 4, 2017, https://www.politifact.com/article/2017/oct/04/mass-shooting-what-does-it-mean/.

8. Jason Silverstein, "There Were More Mass Shootings Than Days in 2019," CBS News, January 2, 2020, www.cbsnews.com/news/mass-shootings-2019-more-than-days-365.

9. "The Evolution of Drug Use in the 21st Century," Dual Diagnosis, accessed June 11, 2020, https://dualdiagnosis.org/the-history-of-drug-abuse-and-how-its-changed.

10. "National Comorbidity Survey," Harvard Medical School, accessed June 11, 2020, www.hcp.med.harvard.edu/ncs.

11. "Why Are More American Teenagers Than Ever Suffering From Severe Anxiety?" Children's Health Council, October 25, 2017, www.chconline.org/american-teenagers-ever-suffering-severe-anxiety.

12. https://www.who.int/docs/default-source/coronaviruse/situation-reports/20200701-covid-19-sitrep-163.pdf?sfvrsn=c202f05b_2

13. Heather Long and Andrew Van Dam, "America Is in a Depression. The Challenge Now Is to Make It Short-Lived," The Washington Post, April 9, 2020, www.washingtonpost.com/business/2020/04/09/66-million-americans-filed-unemployed-last-week-bringing-pandemic-total-over-17-million.

14. Chris Westfall, "The Unseen Unemployed: Why Skyrocketing Unemployment Numbers Are Incomplete," Forbes, May 9, 2020, www.forbes.com/sites/chriswestfall/2020/05/08/the-unseen-unemployed-why-skyrocketing-unemployment-numbers-are-incomplete/#3f71de7f14f5.

15. Annie Nova, "Baby Boomers Face More Risks to Their Retirement Than Previous Generations," CNBC, November 8, 2018, www.cnbc.com/2018/11/07/one-third-of-baby-boomers-had-nothing-saved-for-retirement-at-age-58-.html.

16. "Snowflake Generation Definition and Meaning: Collins English Dictionary," Snowflake generation definition and meaning | Collins English Dictionary (HarperCollins Publishers Ltd), accessed July 10, 2020, https://www.collinsdictionary.com/us/dictionary/english/snowflake-generation.

17. Wikipedia, s.v. "Snowflake (slang)," last modified April 29, 2020, https://en.wikipedia.org/wiki/Snowflake_(slang).

18. Conor Friedersdorf, "The New Intolerance of Student Activism," The Atlantic, November 14, 2015, www.theatlantic.com/politics/archive/2015/11/the-new-intolerance-of-student-activism-at-yale/414810.

19. See Tim Elmore, 12 Huge Mistakes Parents Can Avoid, (Eugene, OR: Harvest House, 2014).

20. Richard Fry, "For First Time in Modern Era, Living With Parents Edges Out Other Living Arrangements for 18- to 34-Year-Olds," Pew Research Center's Social & Demographic Trends Project, May 30, 2020. https://www.pewsocialtrends.org/2016/05/24/for-first-time-in-modern-era-living-with-parents-edges-out-other-living-arrangements-for-18-to-34-year-olds/.

CHAPTER TWO

21. "Folger Library – Churchill's Shakespeare," The International Churchill Society, October 21, 2018, https://winstonchurchill.org/resources/in-the-media/churchill-in-the-news/folger-library-churchills-shakespeare/.

22. History.com Editors, "Spanish Flu," History.com, May 19, 2020, www.history.com/topics/world-war-i/1918-flu-pandemic.

23. History.com Editors, "Spanish Flu."

24. Charles C. Mann, "Pandemics Leave Us Forever Altered," The Atlantic, May 7, 2020, www.theatlantic.com/magazine/archive/2020/06/pandemics-plagues-history/610558.

25. José A. Tapia Granados and Ana V. Diez Roux, "Life and Death During the Great Depression," PNAS, October 13, 2009, www.pnas.org/content/106/41/17290.

26. These results are based on qualitative data not quantitative data from interviews with senior citizens over eighty years old.

27. José A. Tapia Granados and Ana V. Diez Roux, "Life and Death During the Great Depression," PNAS, October 13, 2009, www.pnas.org/content/106/41/17290.

28. Ulrike Malmendier and Stefan Nagel, "Depression Babies: Do Macroeconomic Experiences Affect Risk-Taking?" March 2008, https://doi.org/10.3386/w14813.

29. Sally C. Curtin and Melonie Heron, "Death Rates Due to Suicide and Homicide Among Persons Aged 10–24: United States, 2000–2017," NCHS Data Brief, no. 352 (October 2019), www.cdc.gov/nchs/data/databriefs/db352-h.pdf.

30. Adam Piore, "Gen Zs Are Anxious, Entrepreneurial and Determined to ..." Newsweek Magazine, June 13, 2019, www.newsweek.com/2019/06/28/gen-zs-are-anxious-entrepreneurial-determined-avoid-their-predecessors-mistakes-1443581.html.

31. Piore, "Gen Zs."

32. Ann Stull Ardyth, "Stories of the Children of the Great Depression: What I Learned from My Parents" (graduate dissertation, Iowa State University, 2013), https://lib.dr.iastate.edu/etd/13582.

33. Black Eyed Peas, "Let's Get It Started" (A&M Records, 2004).

34. Twenty One Pilots, "Stressed Out" (Los Angeles: Can Am and London: Livingston Studios, 2015).

35. Chainsmokers, "Sick Boy" (Disruptor Records and Columbia Records, 2018).

36. Gnash, "Pajamas" (Spotify Studios NYC, 2019).

37. Billie Eilish, "Bury a Friend" (Interscope Records, 2020).

38. Monica Moser, "The Issue With Billie Eilish's Darkness," Medium, April 22, 2019, medium.com/@monicamarymoser/the-issue-with-billie-eilishs-darkness-aa2ac8b5349e.

39. Alberto Acerbi, Cultural Evolution in the Digital Age, (London, UK: Oxford University Press, 2019).

40. Myra Interiano, et al., "Musical Trends and Predictability of Success in Contemporary Songs in and out of the Top Charts," Royal Society Open Science 5, no. 5 (2018): https://171274, doi:10.1098/rsos.171274.

41. Emmy E. Werner, Through the Eyes of Innocents Children Witness World War II (Boulder, Colo.: Westview Press, 2011).

42. Diana Divecha, "Will the Pandemic Have a Lasting Impact on My Kids?" Greater Good Magazine, greatergood.berkeley.edu/article/item/will_the_pandemic_have_a_lasting_impact_on_my_kids.

43. Divecha, "Will the Pandemic…?"

44. Divecha, "Will the Pandemic…?"

45. Divecha, "Will the Pandemic…?"

46. Leah Farish, "Encouragement and Prayers for the Graduates in Your Life," EnCourage, April 14, 2020, encourage.pcacdm.org/2020/04/30/post-template-213-26/.

CHAPTER THREE

47. Eric Spitznagel, "Why American Life Went On as Normal During the Killer Pandemic of 1969," New York Post, May 18, 2020, nypost.com/2020/05/16/why-life-went-on-as-normal-during-the-killer-pandemic-of-1969.

48. Jim Poling, Killer Flu: The World on the Brink of a Pandemic, (Altitude Pub., 2006).

49. Eric Spitznagel, "Why American Life."

50. Eric Spitznagel, "Why American Life."

51. Angela Duckworth, Grit (London: Vermilion, 2019).

52. Courtney E. Ackerman, "Learned Helplessness: Seligman's Theory of Depression (+ Cure)," PositivePsychology.com, May 12 2020, https://positivepsychology.com/learned-helplessness-seligman-theory-depression-cure.

53. Julie Beck, "When Do You Become an Adult?" The Atlantic, February 22, 2016, www.theatlantic.com/health/archive/2016/01/when-are-you-really-an-adult/422487.

54. Daniel Coyle, "The Simple Phrase That Increases Effort 40%," December 13, 2013, www.danielcoyle.com/2013/12/13/the-simple-phrase-that-increases-effort-40.

CHAPTER FOUR

55. Ezgi Zeren, "What Did Newton Do with His Time During Quarantine?" Medium, May 30, 2020, https://medium.com/cantors-paradise/what-did-newton-do-with-his-time-during-quarantine-df85c2028e04.

56. Gillian Brockell, "During a Pandemic, Isaac Newton Had to Work from Home, Too. He Used the Time Wisely," The Washington Post, March 12, 2020, www.washingtonpost.com/history/2020/03/12/during-pandemic-isaac-newton-had-work-home-too-he-used-time-wisely.

57. Owen Jarus, "Who Were the Barbarians?," LiveScience (Purch, April 27, 2018), https://www.livescience.com/45297-barbarians.html.

58. Bryan Walsh, "Study Shows That Survivors of the Medieval Plague Were Healthier," Time (Time, May 7, 2014), https://time.com/91315/the-medieval-black-death-made-you-healthier-if-you-survived/.

59. Jim Collins, Good to Great: Why Some Companies Make the Leap … and Others Don't. (New York: Random House, 2001).

60. "The Stockdale Paradox," (audio transcript), Jim Collins, www.jimcollins.com/media_topics/TheStockdaleParadox.html.

61. Karen Given, "'The Monopolists' Uncovers The Origins Of Monopoly." WBUR, February 21, 2015, www.wbur.org/onlyagame/2015/02/21/monopoly-book-mary-pilon.

62. Bruce Lambert, "Alfred M. Butts, 93, Is Dead; Inventor of Scrabble," New York Times, April 7, 1993, www.nytimes.com/1993/04/07/obituaries/alfred-m-butts-93-is-dead-inventor-of-scrabble.html.

CHAPTER FIVE

63. Andy Crouch et al., "Leading Beyond the Blizzard: Why Every Organization Is Now a Startup," The Praxis Journal, April 24, 2020, https://journal.praxislabs.org/leading-beyond-the-blizzard-why-every-organization-is-now-a-startup-b7f32fb278ff.

64. Eric Hoover. "How Is Covid-19 Changing Prospective Students' Plans? Here's an Early Look." The Chronicle of Higher Education, The Chronicle of Higher Education, 25 Mar. 2020, www.chronicle.com/article/How-Is-Covid-19-Changing/248316.

65. Scott Carlson, "Think Student Activists Are 'Snowflakes'? Think Again," The Chronicle of Higher Education, February 16, 2020, www.chronicle.com/article/Think-Student-Activists-Are/248055.

CHAPTER SIX

66. "Millennials Are Getting Stung By Back-To-Back Economic Crises," Financial Advisor, April 8, 2020, www.fa-mag.com/news/millennials-are-getting-stung-by-back-to-back-economic-crises-55087.html.

67. Catherine Bosley, "Millennials Are Getting Stung by Back-to-Back Global Crises," Bloomberg, April 9, 2020, www.bloombergquint.com/global-economics/millennials-are-getting-stung-by-back-to-back-economic-crises.

68. Ben Steverman, "Half of Older Americans Have Nothing in Retirement Savings," Bloomberg, March 26, 2019, www.bloomberg.com/news/articles/2019-03-26/almost-half-of-older-americans-have-zero-in-retirement-savings.

69. Barbara Hoberock, "Governor Faces Social Media Backlash Following Tweet at Eating Establishment," Tulsa World, March 15, 2020, www.tulsaworld.com/news/local/governor-faces-social-media-backlash-following-tweet-at-eating-establishment/article_cbd66825-cad9-5ac4-9e87-1af34b9846b9.html.

70. John Tierney, The Power of Bad (New York: Penguin, 2019), 189–190.

71. Tierney, Power of Bad, 189–190.

72. Tierney, Power of Bad, 190–191.

73. Christine Carter, "How to Help Your Kids Handle the Loss of Graduations and Proms," Ideas.ted.com, May 28, 2020, https://ideas.ted.com/how-to-help-your-kids-handle-the-loss-of-graduations-and-proms.

74. Brené Brown, Daring Greatly: How the Courage to Be Vulnerable Transforms the Way We Live, Love, Parent and Lead, (Avery, 2015).

75. Ann M. Altman et al., "More Than Just a Sugar Pill: Why the Placebo Effect Is Real," Science in the News 14 (Sept. 2016), sitn.hms.harvard.edu/flash/2016/just-sugar-pill-placebo-effect-real.

76. Greg Lukianoff and Jonathan Haidt, The Coddling of the American Mind (New York: Penguin, 2018).

77. Tierney, Power of Bad, 202–206.

78. Mildred George Goertzel and Victor Geortzel, Cradles of Eminence (Tucson, AZ: Great Potential Press, 1964).

79. Dana Schultz, "Meet the 7,000 'Invisible Hands' Delivering Essentials to At-Risk Citizens," 6sqft.com, March 24, 2020, www.6sqft.com/invisible-hands-coronavirus.

80. Matt Ford, "What Caused the Great Crime Decline in the U.S.?" The Atlantic, April 15, 2016, www.theatlantic.com/politics/archive/2016/04/what-caused-the-crime-decline/477408/.

CHAPTER SEVEN

81. George Qiao, "Why Are Asian American Kids Killing Themselves?" Plan A Mag, January 16, 2020, https://planamag.com/why-are-asian-american-kids-killing-themselves.

82. Robert Rosenthal, and Lenore Jacobson, Pygmalion in the Classroom: Teacher Expectation and Pupils Intellectual Development (Carmarthen: Crown House, 2003).

83. Liana Simstrom, "WATCH: Can You Affect Another Person's Behavior with Your Thoughts?" NPR, September 7, 2018, www.npr.org/sections/health-shots/2018/09/07/644530036/watch-can-you-affect-another-persons-behavior-with-your-thoughts.

84. R. Rosenthal and L. Jacobson, "Pygmalion in the Classroom," The Urban Review 3, no. 1 (1968), 16–20.

85. David Scott Yeager et al., "Breaking the Cycle of Mistrust: Wise Interventions to Provide Critical Feedback Across the Racial Divide," Journal of Experimental Psychology: General 143, no. 2 (2014): 804–824, www.apa.org/pubs/journals/releases/xge-a0033906.pdf.

86. Yeager et al., "Breaking the Cycle."

87. Steven Levitt and Stephen Dubner, Freakonomics (New York: Harper, 2007), 150–151.

88. G. L. Cohen and J. Garcia, "Educational Theory, Practice, and Policy and the Wisdom of Social Psychology," Policy Insights from the Behavioral and Brain Sciences 1, no. 1: (2014), 13–20.

89. Pamela Li, "4 Types of Parenting Styles and Their Effects," (infographic), Parenting For Brain, May 31, 2020, www.parentingforbrain.com/4-baumrind-parenting-styles.

90. "Growth Mindset vs. Fixed + Key Takeaways From Dweck's Book," PositivePsychology.com, November 8, 2019, https://positivepsychology.com/growth-mindset-vs-fixed-mindset/.

CHAPTER EIGHT

91. "Create a Narrative to Better Yourself," Psychology Today, Februry 21, 2018, www.psychologytoday.com/us/blog/ritual-and-the-brain/201802/create-narrative-better-yourself.

92. Dan P. McAdams and Kate C. McLean, "Narrative Identity," SAGE Journals, 2013, https://journals.sagepub.com/doi/abs/10.1177/0963721413475622.

93. McAdams and McLean, "Narrative Identity."

94. Newport Oregon Police Department, Facebook, March 14, 2020, www.facebook.com/NewportPolice/posts/10151320062944944.

95. Greg Lukianoff and Jonathan Haidt, The Coddling of the American Mind: How Good Intentions and Bad Ideas Are Setting up a Generation for Failure (New York: Penguin, 2019).

96. "Coronavirus (COVID-19) Frequently Asked Questions," Centers for Disease Control and Prevention, June 2, 2020, www.cdc.gov/coronavirus/2019-ncov/faq.html?CDC_AA_refVal=https%3A%2F%2Fwww.cdc.gov%2Fcoronavirus%2F2019-ncov%2Fprepare%2Fchildren-faq.html.

97. Reis Thebault et al., "How to Prepare for Coronavirus in the U.S." The Washington Post, March 11, 2020, www.washingtonpost.com/health/2020/02/26/how-to-prepare-for-coronavirus/?arc404=true.

98. Reis Thebault (Washington Post), "How to Prepare for Coronavirus in U.S." Times Telegram, February 27, 2020, www.timestelegram.com/news/20200227/how-to-prepare-for-coronavirus-in-us.

99. Greg Nelson, "The Stories You Tell Yourself Matter: Four Steps To Developing An Empowering Narrative," Gregory P. Nelson, August 12, 2014, www.gregorypnelson.com/blog/the-stories-you-tell-yourself-matter-four-steps-to-developing-an-empowering-narrative.

100 "Adverse Childhood Experiences (ACEs)." Centers for Disease Control and Prevention, April 3, 2020, www.cdc.gov/violenceprevention/childabuseandneglect/acestudy/index.html?CDC_AA_refVal=https%3A%2F%2Fwww.cdc.gov%2Fviolenceprevention%2Facestudy%2Findex.html.

101 "When to Rescue and When to Risk With Students," Psychology Today (Sussex Publishers, August 29, 2019), https://www.psychologytoday.com/nz/blog/artificial-maturity/201908/when-rescue-and-when-risk-students.

102 Donna Nakazawa, "7 Ways That Childhood Adversity Can Affect the Brain," Psychology Today, August 7, 2015, www.psychologytoday.com/us/blog/the-last-best-cure/201508/7-ways-childhood-adversity-can-affect-the-brain.

103 Seth Gershenson and Adam Tyner, "Great Expectations: The Impact of Rigorous Grading Practices on Student Achievement," Thomas B. Fordham Institute, April 2, 2020, https://fordhaminstitute.org/national/research/great-expectations-impact-rigorous-grading-practices-student-achievement.

104 "See What Your Friends Are Reading," Goodreads, www.goodreads.com/quotes/6725838-consistent-positive-self-talk-is-unquestionably-one-of-the-greatest-gifts.

105 Shankar Vedantam, Tara Boyle, Laura Kwerel, Parth Shah, Rhaina Cohen, interview with Ayanna Thomas, NPR Hidden Brain, podcast audio, December 16, 2019, https://www.npr.org/2019/12/16/788422090/did-that-really-happen-how-our-memories-betray-us

106 Alexander Kacala, "'What If 2020 Isn't Canceled?' Inspiring Poem with Message of Change Goes Viral," TODAY.com, June 5, 2020, https://www.today.com/news/what-if-2020-isn-t-canceled-inspiring-poem-message-change-t183397.

APPENDIX

107 Carey K. Morewedge, Haewon Yoon, Irene Scopelliti, Carl W. Symborski, James H. Korris, and Karim S. Kassam. "Debiasing Decisions." Policy Insights from the Behavioral and Brain Sciences 2, no. 1 (2015): 129–40. https://doi.org/10.1177/2372732215600886.

108 Daniel Kahneman, "Daniel Kahneman: Beware the "Inside View,"" McKinsey & Company, www.mckinsey.com/business-functions/strategy-and-corporate-finance/our-insights/daniel-kahneman-beware-the-inside-view.

Acknowledgments

I need to acknowledge the team that quickly put this book together:

Andrew McPeak, who's become my "content buddy" and is a constant source of ideas.

Abby Debenedittis, who edited the content and ensured words were clear and correct.

Grace Hooley, who checked the sources and ensured they were accurate.

Cody Braun, who worked to promote and market the content to our audience.

Jim Woodard, who did the layout quickly yet maintained our standard of excellence.

Josh Wood, who created the cover design to align with our brand.

About the Author

Dr. Tim Elmore, Founder & CEO of Growing Leaders, is a best-selling author and international speaker who uses his expertise on generations to equip educators, coaches, leaders, parents, and other adults to impart practical life and leadership skills to young adults that will help them navigate through life.

He educates adults to help them understand the challenges and experiences today's generation faces and connect with them in a way that resonates. Dr. Elmore believes, by cultivating leadership ability in young adults and encouraging the adults who guide them, Growing Leaders can be the catalyst for emerging generations that will truly change the world.

Tim Elmore teaches leadership courses and speaks at schools, universities, businesses, and athletic programs. He has trained thousands of leaders in partnership with nationally renowned schools and organizations like the Kansas City Royals, Stanford University, University of Alabama, National Football League, Ohio State University's Athletic Department, Chick-fil-A, and more.

Dr. Elmore has authored more than 30 books including: *Generation Z Unfiltered: Facing Nine Hidden Challenges of the Most Anxious Population, Habitudes: Images that Form Leadership Habits and Attitudes, Marching Off the Map: Inspire Students to Navigate a Brand New World, Generation iY: Secrets to Connecting with Today's Teens & Young Adults in the Digital Age, 12 Huge Mistakes Parents Can Avoid,* and *Artificial Maturity: Helping Kids Meet the Challenge of Becoming Authentic Adults.*

THE PANDEMIC POPULATION Events

Bring The Pandemic Population to your organization or campus. Hear Dr. Tim Elmore or one of our other amazing speakers share the insights, ideas, and strategies from The Pandemic Population at your next event.

While it's true that today's students present a host of new challenges for those who mentor and lead them, we have hope that they can succeed in life, and like you, we are determined to help them fulfill their potential.

Available as a customized 90-minute, half-day, or full-day presentation, our Pandemic Population in-person or virtual event will further educate your team on the unique characteristics and challenges of Generation Z and provide you with practical strategies to connect with and lead today's young adults after the coronavirus.

We have previously brought Growing Leaders concepts to:

- Schools
- Organizations
- Athletic Departments
- Businesses
- Churches

With the right resources to help educate, lead, and parent young adults better, we can all be a catalyst for emerging generations that will truly change the world.

So, while we all love a good book, this discussion-based workshop can be the catalyst to spark long-term change with your group. We're building a community of leaders to help Generation Z achieve their ultimate potential after the coronavirus. Will you join us?

Contact: Speakers@GrowingLeaders.com

GROWING LEADERS
Ready for Real Life

Imagine a world improved—even transformed—by millions of young influencers who solve problems and serve people in their communities. That's our vision at Growing Leaders.

Founded in 2003 by Dr. Tim Elmore, Growing Leaders is a global non-profit that encourages and equips young adults to take on real-life opportunities and challenges in the classroom, in their careers, and in the community.

We do this by partnering with organizations like yours to teach practical life and leadership skills using real stories, intriguing images, and engaging experiences that are relatable and memorable.

Our process and resources are grounded in research and a unique understanding of the emerging generations, and recognize that leading others at any level begins with learning how to lead yourself.

These tools include:

- Life and leadership skills curriculum to educators and trainers
- Leadership resources for mentoring communities
- Speakers that can travel to your organization or campus

Some of the organizations that use our training resources include:

- National FFA Organization
- Kansas City Royals Baseball Club (minor league affiliates)
- University of Alabama
- Pepperdine University
- Nebraska Department of Education
- The Ohio State University
- Chick-fil-A Restaurants

Tim Elmore and the Growing Leaders team are available to help you invest wisely in the next generation. For more information, please visit:

GrowingLeaders.com

HABITUDES®

IMAGES THAT FORM LEADERSHIP HABITS & ATTITUDES

Every person is faced with unique obstacles and possibilities throughout his or her life. What makes someone a leader is how they manage them and leverage those experiences to positively influence others.

Habitudes is a curriculum and training system that combines images, relatable stories and experiences into leadership lesson plans that resonate with today's young adults, equipping them to navigate through life's challenges and opportunities.

Grounded in established research, they are a fun, creative, and engaging way that helps young adults:

- Take initiative and set the pace to influence others in positive ways.
- Overcome complex problems through creative persistence.
- Capitalize on personal strengths to be career-ready after graduation.
- Develop critical thinking skills that produce better life choices, such as choosing healthy friends, improving study habits, and setting meaningful goals.

Habitudes has been used in over 10,000 schools and organizations across the world for:

- Secondary School Advisement Periods
- Athletic Programs (High School, College, and Professional)
- College Freshmen Programs
- Corporate On-boarding Programs for Young Professionals
- Leadership Classes
- Youth Groups

"Habitudes has it all. It has the implementation of why we're doing this and the why behind 'you should have integrity.' We found something that the kids are hooked on immediately."

\- Julie Diaz, Principal of Travis High School

For a Free Sample visit GrowingLeaders.com/Habitudes